# Beauty Poetry

"She Walks in Beauty"

I0807223

*Titles in the Pure Poetry series:*

**Beauty Poetry:**
**"She Walks in Beauty"**

ISBN 978-0-7660-4243-8

**Death Poetry:**
**"Death, Be Not Proud"**

ISBN 978-0-7660-4257-5

**Love Poetry:**
**"How Do I Love Thee?"**

ISBN 978-0-7660-4284-1

**Nature Poetry:**
**"Make Me a Picture of the Sun"**

ISBN 978-0-7660-4244-5

Pure Poetry

# Beauty Poetry

"She Walks in Beauty"

Sheila Griffin Llanas

Enslow Publishers, Inc.
40 Industrial Road
Box 398
Berkeley Heights, NJ 07922
USA
http://www.enslow.com

**Library of Congress Cataloging-in-Publication Data**

Llanas, Sheila Griffin, 1958–
Beauty poetry : "She walks in beauty" / Sheila Griffin Llanas.
pages cm. — (Pure Poetry)
Includes index.
Summary: "Explores beauty-themed poetry, including famous American and European poets and their poems, as well as literary criticism, poetic technique, explication, and prompts for further study"—Provided by publisher.
ISBN 978-0-7660-4243-8
1. Poetry—History and criticism—Juvenile literature. 2. Beauty, Personal, in literature. 3. Poetry—Authorship—Juvenile literature. I. Title.
PN1111.L53 2014
809.1—dc23 2013013731

Future editions:
Paperback ISBN: 978-1-4644-0429-0
EPUB ISBN: 978-1-4645-1234-6
Single-User PDF ISBN: 978-1-4646-1234-3
Multi-User PDF ISBN: 978-0-7660-5866-8

Printed in the United States of America

112013 Lake Book Manufacturing, Inc., Melrose Park, IL

10 9 8 7 6 5 4 3 2 1

**To Our Readers:** We have done our best to make sure all Internet addresses in this book were active and appropriate when we went to press. However, the author and the publisher have no control over and assume no liability for the material available on those Internet sites or on other Web sites they may link to. Any comments or suggestions can be sent by e-mail to comments@enslow.com or to the address on the back cover.

Enslow Publishers, Inc., is committed to printing our books on recycled paper. The paper in every book contains 10% to 30% post-consumer waste (PCW). The cover board on the outside of each book contains 100% PCW. Our goal is to do our part to help young people and the environment too!

**Photo and Illustration Credits:** Clipart.com, pp. 67, 87; Library of Congress Prints and Photographs, pp. 11, 25, 76, 101; iStockphotos/© 2013 Thinkstock, p. 36; Photos.com/© Getty Images, p. 48; Shutterstock.com, p. 3.

**Cover Illustration:** Shutterstock.com.

# Contents

# Introduction

So many things can be declared beautiful, from tangible objects to intangible ideas and feelings. In many cases, cultural values help establish standards of beauty or aesthetic taste. As values change, so do shared definitions of beauty. Historically, ideas of aesthetics and beauty are often built on or rejected from one era to the next.

During the reign of Queen Elizabeth I, the Renaissance era, from roughly 1450 to 1600, there was a focus on science and humanity's relationship to nature. Landscape painting became a new art form.

The Enlightenment era, from roughly 1600 to 1800, also called the Age of Reason, was a time of enormous scientific discovery. Scientists studied geography, astronomy, and climate, learning the actual, not mythical, causes of natural phenomena. Artists valued accuracy and imitated ancient classical Greek and Roman art.

Then things began to change. The focus shifted away from logic and back to a sense of mystery. The Romantic era, from roughly 1790 to 1860, was a time of psychological exploration. Poets and artists linked their art to human emotions. When they saw beauty, they explored their own passionate responses. This was a new idea, to link an outer image to inner perception. Beauty was not limited only to pleasant images but applied to images that were raw, untamed, and wild—images that triggered extreme emotions, such as terror and horror.

After the Romantic era, ideas of beauty changed again, in the Modern era, from 1890 to the 1940s. When industrialism made the world seem harsh, cold, and even ugly, artists and writers expressed those qualities in their creative work.

Many of the poets represented in this volume wrote during the Romantic era. Their poems reflect their ideas about beauty as well as the cultural attitudes of their time.

At the end of each chapter are five questions. Three short-answer questions require brief responses. If you need help, review the text. Two "ponder further" questions ask you to look beyond the chapter, perhaps to another source, and write a longer answer.

You can also interact with the poems in general ways:

- **Study the poems.** Be patient as you read the poems. Read slowly, just a few lines at a time, if necessary. Read them aloud. Listen to how they sound. These poems are not necessarily easy to read. To help you with your close reading, paraphrase or summarize the key ideas, or write your own version of the poem.

- **Consider the analysis.** As you read a poem's explication, ask yourself whether you agree with it or not. A good analysis, based on a close reading, asserts a reader's opinion. Using the explication as a model, form an interpretation of your own.
- **Make a comparison.** Compare any poem to any one of the other seven poems in the book. When you set them side by side, striking differences will appear. This helps you more clearly understand elements of each poem. Note your observations in a two-column chart or a brief essay.
- **Consider the poet.** Notice biographical details of each poet. Is the poet American or British, a man or a woman? How might these factors influence the work? What details in a poem reflect its author's heritage and background, gender, or social status?

When you close this book, you may find yourself thinking about these poems and the quality of beauty. If you feel inspired to read more, you can find the poets' work online, in the library, or in a bookstore. If you feel inspired to write poetry of your own—perhaps on the theme of beauty—all you need is a place to write down your words.

# 1

# "Sonnet 18"

# William Shakespeare (1564–1616)

William Shakespeare wrote 154 sonnets. There are no records confirming their exact dates, but they may have been written between the years 1592 and 1598. Supposedly, his sonnets were published without his permission in 1609.

Scholars generally agree that the sonnets tell a story of two characters. The narrator, an older male poet, speaks to a younger man he adores and admires. The nature of their relationship is not clear, whether it is a romance, friendship, or mentorship. What is clear is the older poet's love and admiration for the young man.

In the first seventeen sonnets, the poet urges the young man to marry and pass his beauty along to his children. In that way, he claims, the young man will preserve his perfect beauty.

## William Shakespeare

**William Shakespeare is considered England's national poet, and almost nothing is known about him. Biographers have studied his plays and poems to learn about his life. In London, he was very involved in the theater. From 1590 to 1613, he wrote thirty-eight plays and his famous series of sonnets. Shakespeare may have acted in some plays, even taking small parts in his own plays, too. When the Globe Theater opened in 1599, he owned a share in it, along with other actors and playwrights. The Globe burned down in 1613. It was rebuilt the next year and was closed in 1642.**

After begging the young man to have children, beginning with "Sonnet 18," the poet promises to immortalize the man's beauty in poetry. In the final sonnets, the older poet and young man compete for the love of a "dark lady."

Did Shakespeare speak from experience? Some scholars believe his sonnets reflect his real life. One clue supporting this theory is that the speaker discusses writing the sonnets, making them sound autobiographical. Other scholars argue that the sonnets are fictional and that Shakespeare and the speaker of the sonnets are separate. After all, Shakespeare created a flawed speaker, one who is overly confident in some places and fearful in others. The real poet and the character of the older poet are not the same. Or are they?

William Shakespeare

## Sonnet 18

*Shall I compare thee to a summer's day?*
*Thou art more lovely and more temperate*.*
*Rough winds do shake the darling buds of May;*
*And summer's lease hath all too short a date.*
*Sometime too hot the eye of heaven shines,*
*And often is his gold complexion dimm'd;*
*And every fair from fair sometime declines,*
*By chance, or nature's changing course untrimm'd;*
*But thy eternal summer shall not fade,*
*Nor lose possession of that fair thou owest;*
*Nor shall Death brag thou wand'rest in his shade,*
*When in eternal lines to time thou grow'st*
*So long as men can breathe or eyes can see,*
*So long lives this, and this gives life to thee.*

***temperate:** even-tempered; calm

## Summary

"Sonnet 18" is probably the best known of Shakespeare's series. The speaker of the poem, the older poet, poses a question for himself: "Shall I compare thee to a summer's day?" In the next line, he says that his beloved is lovelier than a summer's day. A beautiful day can change. He explains that the weather can turn unpleasant. Winds can shake trees. Summer is too short. The sun, which he calls "the eye of heaven," gets too hot. The sun's "gold complexion" dims if the summer day grows cloudy.

Finally, he decides, "every fair from fair" declines. Everything beautiful grows tarnished. The beauty fades from what is beautiful. Beauty does not last. Suddenly, the poet claims he can make his subject's beauty last. He can write about his love's beauty in poetry. This will immortalize them both.

## Explication

When the speaker asks, "Shall I compare thee to a summer's day?" he focuses on himself, not his subject. He does not ask, "Is your beauty like a summer's day?" He asks if he should make the comparison. He seems to pose the question to himself and wonders if his comparison is a good one. In line 2, he claims it is not. His friend is more beautiful. A summer's day is inferior to his friend's beauty. He spends the next six lines arguing why the comparison is a failure.

Why doesn't the poet describe his subject's beauty? Why does he choose an unfitting comparison? Though his beloved is lovelier than a summer's day, the speaker provides no details to prove his love's beauty is greater. He states many reasons why a summer's day is inferior, however. A summer day represents time, which is unpredictable. Nature itself is constantly changing. A perfect day can turn rotten. Maybe the older poet is trying to make his friend feel wonderful. Mostly, though, he criticizes nature.

By lines 7 and 8, the poet describes nature at its worst. He speaks a truth he cannot handle. Everything beautiful fades, the older poet says, sometimes "By chance, or nature's changing course untrimm'd." Stating it should mean admitting that his beloved will change, too, like nature. People show flaws, grow emotional, and make bad decisions. As much as people love each other, they also hurt those they love. Perhaps worst of all, people age, as the older poet knows well. Because he does not want to see that happen to his young friend, he denies what he knows is true.

"But thy eternal summer shall not fade," he claims, in a desperate and ludicrous boast. In some ways, it is a lie—a promise he cannot guarantee. No one can stop old age and death. No one can stop the powers of nature and time. However, he means that he preserves his friend's beauty in his writing. The speaker dares to think his art has the power to stop time.

Ultimately, the older poet glimpses his own mortality. He was once a young man. Now he is growing old and facing death. He has already proved that "nature's changing course" rarely preserves anything. The answer to his first question, then, is no. "Shall I compare thee to a summer's day?" No, he should not, because people are part of nature, which means their beauty fades. He interrupts this thought process, refusing to follow this line of thinking to its logical conclusion. He changes the subject and takes comfort in art. His poems have a chance to last forever.

One trait of Shakespeare is that he often hides profound messages within simple stories. Humans are controlled, in part, by nature and time. Individuals will die, but humanity will live on, in history, philosophy, art, and societies. In a way, Shakespeare's speaker is not wrong to boast that he can immortalize his love's beauty. Art can survive time. If the older poet wants to capture profound beauty and preserve a human experience from oblivion, his poems are the only means for him to do that.

## Style, Technique, & Poetic Devices

Shakespeare used a popular pattern of his era called the Elizabethan sonnet. Because he was one of the most popular poets to use this form, today it is also referred to as Shakespearean. His lines are written in iambic pentameter, five sets of unstressed and stressed syllables. For example, the rhythm in the first line sounds like this:

1 2 3 4 5
Shall **I** / com-**pare** / thee **to** / a **sum-** / mer's **day**?

Scholars have noted that "I" is stressed while "thee" is unstressed. Even in meter, the older poet exalts his ego over his subject's beauty.

The sonnet is composed of three quatrains, groups of four lines that share a rhyme scheme, and one couplet, a pair of end-rhymed lines. The lines have a pattern of end rhymes, a scheme of *abab cdcd efef gg*. At some point in a sonnet, the poem "turns" or changes direction. The theme gets an unexpected twist. Sometimes, as in "Sonnet 18," Shakespeare places his turn in the third quatrain. In other poems, he waits until the final couplet to deliver the sonnet's surprising turn.

Shakespeare often compared beauty to natural images. Nature was the standard by which to judge beauty. In his first line, "Shall I compare thee to a summer's day?" he introduces a simile, a comparison of two things. But by line 9, the third quatrain, he says, "Thy eternal summer shall not fade!" He has deepened the simile to a metaphor, describing his friend's beauty as not *like* summer, but as if beauty is a real summer. In this way, Shakespeare lets his speaker inadvertently prove that his friend is exactly like summer, even as he denies it.

Shakespeare emphasizes this relationship by giving nature human qualities. Shakespeare personifies summer by giving it sight and clear skin. He calls the sun the "eye of heaven," even though the sun cannot see. He says the sun has a "gold complexion" even though the sun does not have skin or facial expressions. In that way, Shakespeare puts another twist on the comparison of a person to a summer day. He compares a day to a person.

Shakespeare loved twists and turns like these. This is a point where he and the older poet do not seem necessarily the same. The poem's speaker claims that humans are not like summer days, but Shakespeare hints that they are. Shakespeare suggests that his speaker says one thing but thinks another.

## Thematic Relevance

In the first lines of "Sonnet 1," Shakespeare introduces two main themes that he will carry through the series of sonnets. "From fairest creatures we desire increase,/That thereby beauty's rose might never die." One theme is that people always want more, an "increase" of what they like and think is beautiful, such as "fairest creatures." The other theme is that they never want to lose what they love. For example, people do not want roses to die. One way to prevent roses from dying is to grow more roses. One way to increase his friend's beauty is to pass the beauty genes to children. Another way is to write poems about his beloved's beauty.

Shakespeare succeeded. His poems have lasted for centuries, and "Sonnet 18" is one of his most famous sonnets. Because the poet praises himself, not another person, and presumes that his poems will live forever, well after he dies, some critics have called "Sonnet 18" self-glorifying. It is helpful to read other sonnets in the series. The confidence in this poem masks insecurities expressed in others, in which he apologizes for his weak skills.

## Further Study Questions

### Recall Questions

1. The first quatrain has an end-rhymed scheme of *abab*. What are the *a*-words and *b*-words that rhyme?
2. The chapter identifies line 9, "But thy eternal summer shall not fade," as the turn in the sonnet. Why? What ideas lead the speaker to say this line? How does the poem change after this line?
3. What is an example of personification in the poem, one not mentioned in the explication?

**Ponder Further**

4. Shakespeare's sonnets form a series, meant to be read together. Online or in the library, find and read another of Shakespeare's sonnets about beauty, such as "Sonnet 54," "104," or "116." In what ways can you link the sonnet you chose to "Sonnet 18"? What themes and ideas do they share and develop? How are they different?
5. In more recent times, many poets have written sonnet sequences, including Elizabeth Barrett Browning, *Sonnets From the Portuguese* (1850); Christina Rossetti, *Monna Innominata* (1881); and W. H. Auden, "In Time of War" (1939). Using this chapter's explication as a model, find a sonnet that you like by another poet and explicate it.

2

# "To S.M. a Young African Painter, on Seeing His Works"

# Phillis Wheatley

## (1753–1784)

In 1770, Phillis Wheatley wrote a funeral poem for a minister who had died. She was about seventeen years old. Her elegy was printed and reprinted in Boston, New York, Philadelphia, and beyond. This young woman, an enslaved African American, had become famous.

The community took notice. Clergymen and other Boston society members visited her. Selena Hastings, Countess of Huntingdon, a British friend of the deceased minister, supported Wheatley. With her help, a London bookseller printed Wheatley's book *Poems on Various Subjects*, her only published work, in 1773. Lady Huntingdon was the one to request a portrait of Wheatley for the book.

Scipio Moorhead was the artist chosen. Like Wheatley, he was a slave in Boston.

When her book appeared, it bore the lengthy title *Poems on Various Subjects, Religious and Moral by Phillis Wheatley, Negro Servant to Mr. John Wheatley, of Boston, in New England*. Inside was Moorhead's portrait. Moorhead portrayed Wheatley sitting at a writing table. She holds a feather quill pen above a blank page and near an open inkwell. With her finger on her cheek, she gazes upward as if thinking about her next line. Moorhead drew her in the act of writing a poem. Among the thirty-nine poems was her tribute, "To S.M. a Young African Painter, on Seeing His Works."

Wheatley was the first African American, first enslaved person, and third woman in the United States to publish a book of poems. At the time, women had few rights. African Americans had even fewer. Wheatley's skills alarmed and outraged some people. Some questioned the originality of her book. She was a copycat, they said, and a fake. People denied that a female African American could have talent, much less emotions and thoughts of her own.

Wheatley was forced to stand in court as eighteen community leaders, including John Hancock and the governor of Massachusetts, interviewed her. They treated her as if she were on trial. Wheatley trembled in fear. But her impressive answers convinced the men. They signed a document declaring that she had authored the book.

# To S.M. a Young African Painter, on Seeing His Works

*To show the lab'ring bosom's deep intent,*
*And thought in living characters to paint,*
*When first thy pencil did those beauties give,*
*And breathing figures learnt from thee to live,*
*How did those prospects give my soul delight,*
*A new creation rushing on my sight?*
*Still, wondrous youth! each noble path pursue;*
*On deathless glories fix thine ardent* view:*
*Still may the painter's and the poet's fire,*
*To aid thy pencil and thy verse conspire!*
*And may the charms of each seraphic theme*
*Conduct thy footsteps to immortal fame!*
*High to the blissful wonders of the skies*
*Elate thy soul, and raise thy wishful eyes.*
*Thrice happy, when exalted to survey*
*That splendid city, crowned with endless day,*
*Whose twice six gates on radiant hinges ring:*
*Celestial Salem blooms in endless spring.*
*Calm and serene thy moments glide along,*
*And may the muse inspire each future song!*
*Still, with the sweets of contemplation blessed,*
*May peace with balmy wings your soul invest!*
*But when these shades of time are chased away,*
*And darkness ends in everlasting day,*

*On what seraphic pinions* shall we move,*
*And view the landscapes in the realms above?*
*There shall thy tongue in heavenly murmurs flow,*
*And there my muse with heavenly transport glow;*
*No more to tell of Damon's tender sighs,*
*Or rising radiance of Aurora's* eyes;*
*For nobler themes demand a nobler strain,*
*And purer language on the ethereal plain.*
*Cease, gentle Muse! the solemn gloom of night*
*Now seals the fair creation from my sight.*

*__ardent:__ fiery, passionate

*__seraphic pinions:__ angelic wings; also angelic workings

*__Aurora's:__ lights in the night sky, as aurora borealis, or northern lights

## Phillis Wheatley

A young girl, estimated to be seven years old, was captured in West Africa—from Senegal or Gambia—and forced onto a slave ship named the *Phillis*. The girl was weak, small, and frail. The day the ship landed in Boston, Massachusetts, July 11, 1761, the slave trader put a sale price on the girl, hoping to sell her before she died. A wealthy couple, John and Susannah Wheatley, purchased her. They named her Phillis, after the slave ship, and took her to live in their mansion. Phillis Wheatley did the chores of a house servant, but she expressed such an ability to learn that the Wheatleys' eighteen-year-old daughter, Mary, tutored her. Phillis learned to speak English, and she went on to devour books on history, geography, literature, religion, and languages. By age twelve, she was reading Greek and Latin classics. By age thirteen, she had published her first poem.

Phillis Wheatley

## Summary

Wheatley's poem is a form of thanks to another artist. Scipio Moorhead drew Wheatley's portrait, and she wrote a poem for him to return the favor. In doing so, she expresses her beliefs about the timelessness of art.

In her poem, she expresses the surprise and delight of seeing her portrait. His art, "rushing on my sight," makes a strong impact on her. Their artistic exchange, a poem for a painting, connects them. She describes the way the creative process consumes the two of them. As artists, herself as a poet and Scipio as a painter, they should let the noble themes of their work conduct or guide them. She suggests a friendship. She and Scipio can be muses for each other. She inspires him to paint, and he inspires her to write. She expresses a wish that this artistic collaboration lead to "immortal fame."

## Explication

In her tribute to S. M., Phillis Wheatley praises the beauty of art. In her line, "breathing figures learnt from thee to live," she implies that art imitates life, and it also inspires viewers to live. In that way, art is greater than the artists. She promotes the belief that art can be eternal. Much of her poem anticipates a future glory and celebrates a vision of heaven. The artists must wait for death, when "darkness ends in everlasting day," to escape life's darkness and

# Growing Up a Slave

In spite of Phillis Wheatley's remarkable literary achievements, she never experienced social equality. Her owners treated her well, caring for her health, educating her, and encouraging her to write, but Wheatley was still a house slave. As such, she was expected to defer to all of white society.

Her poems, however, reveal little about her station as a slave. Scholars and critics have suggested that slavery must have shaped her self-identity. In the twentieth century, some critics challenged Wheatley for not expressing her African heritage or taking a stance against slavery. Why didn't she express outrage over racial injustice, even in veiled terms?

Scholars, artists, and writers continue to consider these questions. Alice Walker's *In Search of Our Mothers' Gardens* and Henry Louis Gates, Jr., in *The Trials of Phillis Wheatley: America's First Black Poet and Her Encounters With the Founding Fathers*, share the belief that Phillis Wheatley has been misunderstood over time. Nikki Giovanni, who dedicated her poem "Linkage" to Wheatley, has also defended her.

In Wheatley's time, Boston had few slaves compared to other areas of the United States. She did not experience the brutalities of slavery. She also did not live within a community of other African Americans. Phillis genuinely loved the Wheatley family and had deep faith in Christianity. She appeared to accept a culture that enslaved her. Because of these seeming contradictions and because her writing survived, scholars and poets, such as Walker, Giovanni, and Gates, have come to embrace Wheatley as an important figure in African-American literary history.

to understand eternity and immortality. In creating art, however, artists get a glimpse of eternity. She celebrates the process in her three-part poem.

First, in lines 1 to 6, she sees Moorhead's portrait of her. She is astonished and delighted. Moorhead has portrayed Wheatley in the act of creating. It may be her favorite state of mind. That is when her soul feels exalted and free. She exalts this inspired state of creating, when new ideas come "rushing on my sight!" Moorhead has drawn her intentions and her thoughts. He has captured her artistic talents. She calls these qualities "beauties." In turn, she praises Moorhead's ability to be inspired to make art. In lines 7 to 12, beginning with the phrase "Still, wondrous youth!" she praises his skills, not his painting. For her, the beauty of art is in creating it. She calls the pursuit of art a "noble path." An artist's impulse to create is described as a "fire," a burning inside, with an "ardent view." It is the way that artists achieve "immortal fame."

The couplet in lines 13 and 14 starts the poem's epiphany, the high spot or the peak of the poem. Lines 13 and 14 describe what she saw in the moments of inspiration, when she raised her eyes, the way Scipio Moorhead drew her. She says:

*High to the blissful wonders of the skies*
*Elate thy soul, and raise thy wishful eyes.*

For Wheatley, creative inspiration feels like flying away from reality. Inspiration uplifts her spirit, intellect, and soul. Lines 15 to 22 express the most exultant ideas of the poem. As artists seek higher understanding, as she says in line 15, they are "exalted to survey," to see great sights from a higher point of view. From there, she has a vision of greatness, with qualities of peace, calm, and serenity. "May peace with balmy wings your soul invest!" It is a beautiful wish for another artist.

After that, her poem begins to fall. The energy drains away. Line 23 begins with the word "But." A change happens, and her vision is over. She returns to reality. She begins talking about "shades of time" and the darkness of life. Now she and Moorhead must view the upper realms again from below. She wonders what "seraphic pinions," or angelic wings, will help inspire her creativity. The imagination carried the artist above reality. In the final couplet, she begs the muse to stop. She returns to the idea of darkness. Her creativity is once again hidden, for now.

Moorhead captured Wheatley in the act of creating art. Wheatley's poem captures the three-part process of making art. Inspiration strikes. The artist creates. The inspiration fades. Then the human artists must go on with their daily lives. However, in the artwork itself, the experience of reaching imaginative heights is preserved forever.

# Style, Technique, & Poetic Devices

Wheatley's poem, like much of her work, reveals her strengths as a reader and scholar of poetry. In this poem, she uses several classical allusions, referencing stories from the Bible and Greek mythology. When she mentions "Celestial Salem," in line 18, she may be referring to "Lights Abode, Celestial Salem," a church hymn written in the 1400s that exalts the glories of heaven. Likewise, with her phrase "Damon's tender sighs," Wheatley refers to a Greek myth about two friends, Damon and Pythias, each of whom tried to protect the other from a false sentence of prison and execution. The power of her references adds power to her poem.

Wheatley's poem is built of heroic couplets. Written in iambic pentameter, the form of each pair of end-rhymed lines is closed, meaning they form a single complete thought and come to a grammatical end. Though a few of Wheatley's couplets are open, grammatically flowing into the next lines, most are closed.

Geoffrey Chaucer used heroic couplets in the fourteenth century. In the seventeenth and eighteenth centuries, such poets as John Dryden (1631–1700) and Alexander Pope (1688–1744) used the form in their work and to translate the works of Virgil and Homer. Wheatley's use of heroic

## Connection to History

**In 1775, Wheatley wrote a poem for George Washington, then an army general in the American Revolution. The last four lines are triumphant:**

> ***Proceed, great chief, with virtue on thy side,***
> ***Thy ev'ry action let the Goddess guide.***
> ***A crown, a mansion, and a throne that shine,***
> ***With gold unfading, WASHINGTON! Be thine.***

**She sent her poem to General Washington with a letter full of modesty, in the tradition of her time. "The fame of your virtues," she wrote, "excite sensations not easy to suppress."**

**Washington wrote a personal letter in return, saying that he would publish the poem except that it would make him appear vain. Her patriotic poem was printed many times.**

couplets suggests that she studied and greatly admired these poets, their work, and their translations.

## Thematic Relevance

From a historical perspective, it is astonishing that Phillis Wheatley was encouraged to write and publish her work. In her time, most enslaved people were forbidden to learn to read and write. In her poetry, Wheatley framed qualities as beautiful—moral values, religious faith, and virtues such as humility, modesty, and kindness. In the era of the American Revolution, she appealed to Puritan values.

Many of Wheatley's poems paid tribute to public figures of her day. Some championed her work, such as George Washington and Benjamin Franklin. Other leaders, such as Thomas Jefferson, dismissed and condemned it. In his speech, "Notes on the State of Virginia: Laws," Jefferson defamed Wheatley, saying, "The compositions published under her name are below the dignity of criticism." Jefferson, who was pro-slavery, could never accept the intellectual work of an African-born person. It would have meant admitting to the humanity of African people. In turn, this would have supported the argument to dissolve the institution of slavery. Some historians believe that the Boston community's acceptance of Wheatley's work fueled a growing belief that African Americans should be free and treated as equals.

The Wheatley family granted Phillis her freedom in 1774. Her life as a freed person on her own was much harder than her life as a slave in the Wheatley family mansion. She married, but she and her husband struggled to earn money. She gave birth to three children, all of whom died in infancy. Weak, sick, and living in poverty, Wheatley died at age thirty-one. She had written a second book, but it was never published, and the poems have been lost.

# Further Study Questions

## Recall Questions

1. What qualities did Wheatley consider beautiful? Why?
2. Who was the S. M. in the poem's title? Study his portrait of Phillis Wheatley. What do you notice about the style of the art? Jot down a list of observations.
3. What do lines 21 and 22 mean? Summarize the idea in the couplet, "Still, with the sweets of contemplation blessed / May peace with balmy wings your soul invest!" Put the lines into your own words.

## Ponder Further

4. How do the two art forms, painting and poetry, express ideas similarly or differently? In a brief essay or paragraph, use Wheatley's poem and Scipio Moorhead's portrait as examples.
5. Search for a poem that you like by a contemporary African-American poet, such as Alice Walker, Nikki Giovanni, Rita Dove, or Maya Angelou. Compare and contrast the contemporary poem to the poem by Phillis Wheatley. How much of their differences have to do with their historical context?

# 3

# "She Walks in Beauty"

## Lord Byron (1788–1824)

Lord Byron was short, walked with a limp, and fretted about his weight. He was also considered handsome, flamboyant, and witty. In the public eye, he was dashing, rakish, rebellious, and fashionable. His friend Lady Caroline Lamb wrote in her journal that Byron was "mad, bad, and dangerous to know." His admirers imitated his style. He became tremendously popular in his time.

Byron's poetry had the emotional passion of the Romantic era, but he also used the sarcasm, irony, and cynicism of the early Enlightenment period. His first two books, *Fugitive Pieces* (1806) and *Hours of Idleness* (1807), reveal his tastes in pre-Romantic poets such as Thomas Gray, Robert Burns, and, his favorite, Alexander Pope. Byron often used couplets as Pope did. The first six lines

## Lord Byron

**George Gordon Noel Byron was born on January 22, 1788, in London. Because his family had a noble title but no money, Byron did not have an easy childhood. He underwent painful treatments to correct a club foot, a birth disorder that caused one foot to turn in, giving him a slight limp. To compensate, he practiced fencing, swimming, and other sports to build his strength. He lived for his first years with his mother in Aberdeen, Scotland. They returned to England in 1798, when, at age ten, he inherited the title of 6th Baron Byron from his great-uncle. The title came with estates but no money. His eccentric great-uncle, who was called "the Wicked Lord," had wasted the inheritance. Byron especially loved Newstead Abbey, his estate in Nottinghamshire, even though the enormous house was in a state of disrepair.**

of one of Byron's early poems, "To Woman," illustrate his skill at rhyme and meter and his taste in humor:

> *Woman! experience might have told me*
> *That all must love thee, who behold thee:*
> *Surely experience might have taught*
> *Thy firmest promises are nought;*
> *But, plac'd in all thy charms before me,*
> *All I forget, but to* adore *thee.*

As he presumes to describe womankind, Byron humorously allows his speaker to reveal the effect a woman's beauty has on him. The emphasis is on a *response* to beauty, not beauty itself, a theme Byron would explore in "She Walks in Beauty."

Lord Byron

# She Walks in Beauty

*SHE walks in beauty, like the night*
*Of cloudless climes* and starry skies;*
*And all that's best of dark and bright*
*Meet in her aspect* and her eyes;*
*Thus mellowed to that tender light*
*Which heaven to gaudy* day denies.*

*One shade the more, one ray the less,*
*Had half impaired the nameless grace*
*Which waves in every raven* tress,*
*Or softly lightens o'er her face;*
*Where thoughts serenely sweet express,*
*How pure, how dear their dwelling-place.*

*And on that cheek, and o'er that brow,*
*So soft, so calm, yet eloquent*,*
*The smiles that win, the tints that glow,*
*But tell of days in goodness spent,*
*A mind at peace with all below,*
*A heart whose love is innocent!*

***climes:** climate; also region (from the Latin word *clima*)

***aspect:** appearance, quality—her facial expression and / or her

***overall** appearance

***gaudy:** garish, overly decorated, cheap-looking

***raven: a** shiny black color

***eloquent:** expressive, usually in terms of speech, but also in action

## Summary

One night, in June 1814, Lord Byron attended a party in South Derbyshire. The host was Byron's cousin, Robert Wilmot-Horton. The man's wife, Anne Beatrix Wilmot-Horton, wore a black velvet dress with silver sequins. As the story goes, her beauty mesmerized Byron. He was astonished by the contrast of her dark hair against her pale skin. He became indrawn and quiet. At home, he could not sleep. He could not stop thinking about her.

The next day, he wrote "She Walks in Beauty." His poem describes a woman in abstract terms, comparing her beauty to night. Around her dark hair and pale face, light and shadows blend in equal measure. It is as if her beauty resulted from the equation. Byron describes her as a woman not merely beautiful but ethereal, with an inner beauty reflected in her eyes, face, and composure. In the final stanza, he suggests that her exterior physical beauty reflects inner virtues and qualities. Byron published the poem in 1815 in his book *Hebrew Melodies*.

## Explication: A Reflection of Light and Dark

Byron defines the woman as beautiful in a very poetic way. She is not merely beautiful. In the first line alone, three aspects make her beauty exceptional and unearthly.

"She walks" makes her an active traveler. "She walks in beauty" makes the quality of beauty seem like a place, not a concept. "She walks in beauty like the night" implies that nature is also in motion, walking in an unearthly beauty that is without limits. An individual inspired the poem. Byron gives her a lofty radiance, with refined intelligence, composure, and emotions. However, the poem is not about a specific woman. It is about beauty itself and what happens when inner and outer beauty are in perfect balance.

"She Walks in Beauty" is a poem of contrasts. In its three stanzas, Byron juxtaposes night and day, heaven and earth, dark and bright, and body and mind. In his most famous line, Byron balances dark and light: "And all that's best of dark and bright/Meet in her aspect and her eyes . . ." Inside and out, the woman has the "best" of both. With balance, she has "tender light." Byron does not equate light with goodness and darkness with evil. In fact, her beauty must be seen at night, not by "gaudy" daylight. By day, she might look like an ordinary individual rather than a goddess walking among stars.

In the second stanza, Byron explains this blend as if it is a formula or an equation. His analysis almost sounds clinical. If she had even one shade more of light or dark, he muses in lines 7 and 8, the effect would be "impaired" or ruined. Seeing her in a perfect balance of light and dark, Byron can imagine she has perfect inner qualities, too. Her eyes, he believes, reveal clear thoughts. Her thoughts reflect the serenity of her mind: "How pure, how dear their dwelling-place." She does not have doubts, worries, or even petty thoughts.

In stanza three, the speaker finally mentions his subject's cheek and brow, but he is careful not to create a specific image. In a poem about beauty, it is odd that Byron never reveals a clue about the woman's physical appearance. He does not want to show the reader what she looks like. His poem is not about a flat picture of a single woman. He distances the woman from himself, in stanza three, by assuming that her actions are good, her mind is at peace, and her love is innocent. Before, he blended dark and bright. Is Byron saying that because the woman is so beautiful, she must be morally good? He ends the poem with her goodness. By isolating her imagined virtues, does he imply his own contrasting vices?

Byron never interacts with his subject. In addition, after the opening two words "she walks," the subject performs no other human actions. She is distant, like a star. Perhaps Byron wants the idea of a beauty this powerful to tantalize the reader the way it did him. Beauty is elusive, something he can barely describe. He can barely stand to look at it. Byron never declares love or infatuation for his subject. He does not want to desire her. He wants to be in awe of her. If her beauty is figuratively like night, it will be cold and distant, after all. Night may be clear and full of stars, but it is still dark, and dark is wild, frightening, and unpredictable.

# Style, Technique, & Poetic Devices

Many readers find "She Walks in Beauty" to be Byron's loveliest lyric poem. Short and simple in form, it has a mathematical balance and an intensity of personal emotion. A single idea controls each stanza. Each of the three stanzas has six lines, broken (more or less) into three phrasings of two lines each. Written mainly in iambic tetrameter, each line has four feet, or pairs of unstressed and stressed syllables.

˘ / ˘ / ˘ / ˘ /
She **walks** in **beau** - ty, **like** the **night**

˘ / ˘ / ˘ / ˘ /
Of **cloud** - less **climes** and **star** - ry **skies**.

The end-rhymed pattern is clear. The words at the end of each line form exact rhymes. *Night* rhymes with *bright*. *Skies* rhymes with *eyes*. Each stanza has the rhyme scheme of *ababab*. The end rhymes are simple, mostly single syllable words.

Though his rhyme and meter have obvious clarity, Byron's internal rhyme gives the poem its soft music. End rhyme is conspicuous; internal rhyme is made when words close to each other in a line or in the poem sound similar. Like a candle in a room, internal rhyme gives the poem a warm glow. Slant rhymes (also called half or near rhymes), placed close together, sound similar but not exact. They share consonant sounds, vowel sounds, or both. The rhyme of *climes* and *skies*, in linc 2, is slant. Sharing the hard "c," long "i," and end "s," the rhyme is close but not exact. The words "cloudless climes" share a hard "c." Paired with "starry skies," all four words share a soft and lulling sibilance. The second stanza, the middle of the poem, is full of such soft sounds, as if the speaker has entered a trance describing the quality of beauty.

Every line has a lot going on. The effect of Byron's internal slant rhyme and alliteration is subtle and powerful. His internal rhymes do not dominate the poem. Rather, they work a soft magic on the reader, as if music is playing in the background. The music creates the poem's gentle undertone.

## Thematic Relevance

Some people believe Byron must have been infatuated with his cousin's wife. His poem proves that he admired her, but he never confesses love for her. "She Walks in Beauty" is not a love poem. Byron showered the subject of his poem with qualities he did not possess, if stories of his notorious behavior are true. Byron allegedly had numerous affairs, some scandalous. Perhaps that is why he ended the poem declaring that the woman enjoyed "days in goodness spent,/A mind at peace with all below,/A heart whose love is innocent!" That was not Byron.

Some critics have called Byron's famous line, "all that's best of dark and bright," an accurate description of himself. He did not shy away from his own dark side. The word "best" is a value term. If there is a best, he implies that there is also a worst of dark and bright. Byron was fascinated by the contrast between darkness and light, between the seemingly good and seemingly bad.

Though he defined beauty on its own, he often found it in women. Lord Byron wrote many poems about women whose beauty he admired. He was fourteen when a cousin, Margaret Parker, died. Her passing inspired him to write, "On the Death of a Young Lady." In one of the poem's six quatrains, he visits her grave and comments that her beauty and virtue could not save her from dying.

*Within this narrow cell reclines her clay,*
*That clay, where once such animation beam'd;*
*The King of Terrors seized her as his prey,*
*Not worth, nor beauty, have her life redeem'd.*

In 1821 and 1822, Byron kept a diary for a few months. In one entry, he called his cousin "the most beautiful of evanescent beings." In another entry, he described her again: "I do not recollect scarcely any thing equal to the *transparent* beauty of my cousin, or to the sweetness of her temper, during the short period of our intimacy. She looked as if she had been made out of a rainbow—all beauty and peace."

From 1813 to 1819, Lord Byron wrote and published prolifically. "She Walks in Beauty" is not a humorous poem. However, readers can still recognize Byron's style in the long humorous and satiric poems that are now considered his masterpieces. When Byron traveled to Greece and Turkey, he recorded his experiences in his long poem *Childe Harold's Pilgrimage*. In the poem, his speaker grows tired of seeking pleasure and wants deeper meaning in his life. In 1812, Byron became instantly famous when he published the first two cantos, or sections, of his epic poem. He published the rest of the poem over the next six years.

From 1819 until his death in 1824, Byron worked on *Don Juan*, an epic poem that puts a comical twist on a legend, turning a womanizer into one too easily seduced by women. The satire highlights his cutting sense of humor. In the fifth canto, the narrator describes a woman whom Don Juan has encountered:

*Her presence was as lofty as her state;*
*Her beauty of that overpowering kind,*
*Whose force description only would abate:*
*I'd rather leave it much to your own mind,*
*Than lessen it by what I could relate*
*Of forms and features; it would strike you blind*
*Could I do justice to the full detail;*
*So, luckily for both, my phrases fail.*

In this stanza, in relation to a woman's beauty, Byron again describes not beauty itself but its effect on men.

# Further Study Questions

**Recall Questions**

1. What are two words that share a slant rhyme in the poem? Find an example not mentioned in the chapter.
2. Shakespeare compared his subject to "a summer's day." Byron's subject is "like the night." How are the similes of beauty the same and different?
3. What is the thesis, or main point, of the chapter's explication of the poem?

**Ponder Further**

4. Consider another viewpoint of the poem not discussed in the chapter. If you were going to analyze this poem, what might be your thesis statement?
5. In the library or online, search for an image of Lord Byron. Only paintings exist. There are no photographs of the poet. What qualities do images of him suggest?

4

# "Hymn to Intellectual Beauty"

# Percy Bysshe Shelley (1792–1822)

In 1816, Percy Bysshe Shelley (his middle name is pronounced *Bish*) spent the summer near Lake Geneva, in Switzerland. Joining him were his wife, Mary Shelley, Mary's sister Jane, and their friend Lord Byron. The mountainous scenery enchanted Shelley. He found the Alps exquisitely beautiful. That summer, when Mary Shelley began writing her novel *Frankenstein*, Percy Shelley wrote "Hymn to Intellectual Beauty." On December 8, 1816, Shelley wrote a letter to his friend Leigh Hunt, stating that his poem was "composed under the influence of feelings which agitated me even to tears."

Shelley, like many Romantics, believed poets had a higher calling than simply to entertain readers. Poets revealed truths about life, society,

## Percy Bysshe Shelley

**In college, Shelley's nickname was "Mad Shelley." He was an independent thinker and free spirit, interested in everything—philosophy, politics, religion, classic literature, and science. He lasted a year at Oxford. He and his friend Thomas Jefferson Hogg were expelled for publishing an essay called *The Necessity for Atheism*.**

**Later, Hogg wrote a memoir of those days, called "Shelley at Oxford." It was printed as a series in the *New Monthly Magazine* in 1832 and 1833. According to Hogg, class lectures bored Shelley. He stayed in his rooms, reading and conducting experiments. His clean, freshly painted dorm rooms soon grew cluttered with clothing, writing materials, and scientific instruments, such as, Hogg wrote, "[a]n electrical machine, an air-pump, the galvanic trough, a solar microscope and large glass jars." Chemicals stained the tables and carpets, as well as Shelley's hands and clothes. "He often rose, paced slowly about the room, shook his long, wild locks and discoursed in a solemn tone and with a mysterious air," Hogg wrote, "speculating concerning our previous condition, and the nature of our life and occupations in that world . . . "**

and humanity. Poets were visionaries, and Shelley believed the imagination was the source of visionary creativity. He came to believe in the existence of unseen powers. He believed that human perception was veiled. Beauty had the power to reveal itself in everyday life and ordinary things. In those unexpected moments, Shelley experienced heightened levels of consciousness. He was struck with awe and wonder. Inspired, he wrote during or after these profound experiences. These moments of transcendence seemed beyond his control.

Percy Bysshe Shelley

# Hymn to Intellectual Beauty

*The awful shadow of some unseen Power*
*Floats though unseen among us,—visiting*
*This various world with as inconstant* wing*
*As summer winds that creep from flower to flower,—*
*Like moonbeams that behind some piny mountain shower,*
*It visits with inconstant glance*
*Each human heart and countenance*;*
*Like hues and harmonies of evening,—*
*Like clouds in starlight widely spread,—*
*Like memory of music fled,—*
*Like aught* that for its grace may be*
*Dear, and yet dearer for its mystery.*

*Spirit of BEAUTY, that dost consecrate**
*With thine own hues all thou dost shine upon*
*Of human thought or form,—where art thou gone?*
*Why dost thou pass away and leave our state,*
*This dim vast vale of tears, vacant and desolate?*
*Ask why the sunlight not for ever*
*Weaves rainbows o'er yon mountain-river,*
*Why aught should fail and fade that once is shown,*
*Why fear and dream and death and birth*
*Cast on the daylight of this earth*
*Such gloom,—why man has such a scope*
*For love and hate, despondency and hope?*

*No voice from some sublimer world hath ever*
*To sage or poet these responses given—*
*Therefore the names of Demon, Ghost, and Heaven,*
*Remain the records of their vain endeavour,*
*Frail spells whose utter'd charm might not avail to sever,*
*From all we hear and all we see,*
*Doubt, chance and mutability.*
*Thy light alone like mist o'er mountains driven,*
*Or music by the night-wind sent*
*Through strings of some still instrument,*
*Or moonlight on a midnight stream,*
*Gives grace and truth to life's unquiet dream.*

*Love, Hope, and Self-esteem, like clouds depart*
*And come, for some uncertain moments lent.*
*Man were immortal and omnipotent,*
*Didst thou, unknown and awful as thou art,*
*Keep with thy glorious train firm state within his heart.*
*Thou messenger of sympathies,*
*That wax and wane in lovers' eyes—*
*Thou, that to human thought art nourishment,*
*Like darkness to a dying flame!*
*Depart not as thy shadow came,*
*Depart not—lest the grave should be,*
*Like life and fear, a dark reality.*

*While yet a boy I sought for ghosts, and sped*
*Through many a listening chamber, cave and ruin,*
*And starlight wood, with fearful steps pursuing*
*Hopes of high talk with the departed dead.*
*I call'd on poisonous names with which our youth is fed;*
*I was not heard—I saw them not—*
*When musing deeply on the lot*
*Of life, at that sweet time when winds are wooing*
*All vital things that wake to bring*
*News of birds and blossoming,—*
*Sudden, thy shadow fell on me;*
*I shriek'd, and clasp'd my hands in ecstasy!*

*I vow'd that I would dedicate my powers*
*To thee and thine: have I not kept the vow?*
*With beating heart and streaming eyes, even now*
*I call the phantoms of a thousand hours*
*Each from his voiceless grave: they have in vision'd bowers**
*Of studious zeal* or love's delight*
*Outwatch'd with me the envious night—*
*They know that never joy illum'd my brow*
*Unlink'd with hope that thou wouldst free*
*This world from its dark slavery,*
*That thou, O awful LOVELINESS,*
*Wouldst give whate'er these words cannot express.*

*The day becomes more solemn and serene*
*When noon is past—there is a harmony*
*In autumn, and a lustre in its sky,*
*Which through the summer is not heard or seen,*
*As if it could not be, as if it had not been!*
*Thus let thy power, which like the truth*
*Of nature on my passive youth*
*Descended, to my onward life supply*
*Its calm—to one who worships thee,*
*And every form containing thee,*
*Whom, SPIRIT fair, thy spells did bind*
*To fear himself, and love all human kind.*

*__inconstant:__ random

*__countenance:__ face and facial expression

*__aught:__ nothing

*__consecrate:__ make holy; bless

*__bowers:__ shelters or places of retreat

*__zeal:__ enthusiasm

"Poetry lifts the veil from the hidden beauty of the world," Shelley wrote in his essay *A Defence of Poetry*. "Poetry is a mirror which makes beautiful that which is distorted."

## Summary

The narrator describes an unseen power. This force comes from a sublime place. It randomly visits nature and people. The narrator has trouble describing it. The force is like nothing else. He calls it the "Spirit of Beauty" and wants to know why it leaves. Its absence makes human beings suffer. Occasionally, the Spirit of Beauty reveals itself in nature or humanity. It appears "[a]s summer winds that creep from flower to flower," as well as visiting "[e]ach human heart and countenance." However, this force is invisible and separate from both nature and humanity. When it passes away, it leaves people "vacant and desolate."

Shelley begs the Spirit of Beauty to visit him, "one who worships thee . . ." He longs to know more about the power. Where does it hide? Why does it disappear? Why do people only get glimpses of it? He knows he will get no answer. People are not allowed to be all-knowing. If this force was always present, humans would be "immortal and omnipotent." He begs the spirit not to leave the world. Without it, death would be "a dark reality."

In stanza 5, the narrator tells a story based on an autobiographical event from Shelley's life. When he was young, he tried to see ghosts and speak to the dead. Like many children, he wanted to have fun and scare himself. Instead, he had a spiritual experience of expansive freedom. When, as he says, the shadow of the Spirit of Beauty fell on him, he felt ecstasy. In stanza 6, the narrator dedicates himself to this Spirit. In stanza 7, older, he prays that the power will bring calm to his life. He believes the Spirit of Beauty can free people and save the world. It has taught him to "love all human kind."

## Explication

Shelley's poem is a hymn. He worships what he calls "Intellectual Beauty," whatever that may be. The narrator felt this Spirit of Beauty as a young boy. He knows it exists, and the experience changed his life. The irony is that Shelley is not feeling the Spirit of Beauty when he writes this poem. He is not creatively inspired by it, not in that ecstatic state that is the gift of the Spirit of Beauty. He describes it from memory in a state of longing, missing the Spirit of Beauty.

The narrator attempts to define a force that he knows he will never be able to define. The unseen power is powerful because it is so rarely seen. It is a paradox. The speaker tries to explain something he can hardly understand. This makes the poem a challenge to read! He cannot even describe it, though he tries, in the first stanza, with five images—summer winds, moonbeams, sunset, clouds, and memory of music. None of them fully captures the unseen power. In the last lines of the first stanza, he admits that the power is like nothing. It is dear, or precious, because it is mysterious. He hates that he cannot feel the power all the time, but he knows that if he felt it all the time, he would not revere it.

In stanza 2, he asks questions. If the Spirit of Beauty makes nature beautiful and people happy, why does it leave nature in darkness and people in states of fear and depression? In stanza 3, he answers himself. Human beings have always asked the same questions and have never gotten direct answers. People can only try their best to ward off things such as "Doubt, chance and mutability." They can only wait for, as the narrator expresses in the next five lines, moments of beauty in mist, mountains, music, moonlight, and midnight streams. Again, Shelley uses mysterious nature imagery.

The power of beauty gives the fullest human qualities, "Love, Hope, and Self-esteem," and it is agony that these qualities slip away. The narrator longs to experience this beauty permanently, but his human state prevents it. The narrator realizes that "Intellectual Beauty" hides within himself, connected to his imagination. He cannot feel the power all the time. All he can do is worship it. He begins to revere his imagination.

The narrator attaches the idea of Beauty to nothing in the poem but his imagination. His concept of beauty is abstract, not concrete. Because beauty is an emotional experience, Shelley used vague images, difficult for readers to visualize. Shelley believed beauty was a power hidden within earthly and human nature. He also believed that this power was impossible to understand. He wrote "Hymn to Intellectual Beauty" to express both of those ideas.

## Style, Technique, & Poetic Devices

To address a mystery that has no form, Shelley used a strict, complex form. He gave himself a challenge. In seven stanzas, he wrote an eighty-four-line ode, a poem to express a noble feeling. Each twelve-line stanza has an end-rhymed scheme of *abbaaccbddee*. His lines are written in iambs, or feet, which are pairs of unstressed and stressed syllables. Lines 1 to 4 are in iambic pentameter, with five feet. Line 5 is in hexameter, with six feet. Lines 6 to 11 are iambic tetrameter, with four beats. Finally, line 12 is again in iambic pentameter. Each stanza follows this same highly regular metric scheme.

He uses the rhetorical device of personification. He speaks to a mystery as if it had shape. He pleads with the unseen power even though it has no state of being. When he tries to pinpoint it exactly, he fails. He can only describe what it might be like. None of his five similes, in the first stanza, fully define the "unseen Power."

Some critics have suggested that Shelley needed restrictive rhyme and meter to talk about a wild, powerful force. The rigid form contrasts with the slippery, unreal topic. He attempts to describe something almost impossible to describe. Limiting himself to rigid, strict meters and rhymes helped him structure his chaotic thoughts.

## Thematic Relevance

Shelley defined beauty as a universal, fleeting experience rather than as aesthetic taste. For Shelley, beauty was not in outer objects. Beauty was an experience that could be felt. For that reason, Shelley was able to see artistic beauty in depraved and unpoetic situations. He wrote a poem called, "On the Medusa of Leonardo da Vinci in the Florentine Gallery." The Medusa, in Greek mythology, is a monster. With a woman's face and snakes for hair, she turns anyone who sees her into stone. Shelley describes da Vinci's painting as having a terrifying beauty:

*It lieth, gazing on the midnight sky,*
*Upon the cloudy mountain peak supine;*
*Below, far lands are seen tremblingly;*
*Its horror and its beauty are divine.*
*Upon its lips and eyelids seems to lie*
*Loveliness like a shadow, from which shrine,*
*Fiery and lurid, struggling underneath,*
*The agonies of anguish and of death.*

Readers will recognize themes similar to "Hymn to Intellectual Beauty" in his important poem "Ode to the

West Wind." In the first lines, Shelley addresses another unseen power, this one in nature:

*O wild West Wind, thou breath of Autumn's being,*
*Thou, from whose unseen presence the leaves dead*
*Are driven, like ghosts from an enchanter fleeing . . .*

Some critics found Shelley sentimental and impulsive, a poet who indulged his imagination too much. Others found him to be a great thinker who explored fundamental questions about life and human nature. He thought deeply about the mysteries of the universe.

Shelley's reading of the Greek philosopher Plato may have influenced his idealism. "The Spirit of Solitude" is considered his first major poem. His next important poem was "Hymn to Intellectual Beauty." Some critics have called the poem a statement of his Platonism.

Many of Shelley's poems can be so complex that they are difficult to interpret. His images, word choices, and ideas create as much mystery as the unseen powers of the nonphysical realm he tries to describe.

Influenced by William Wordsworth, Shelley wrote his long poem *Queen Mab*, in 1813. When John Keats died in 1821, Shelley wrote "Adonais" as an elegy for his friend. Shelley's work inspired poets Robert Browning, Dante Gabriel Rossetti, Algernon Charles Swinburne, Lord Alfred Tennyson, and William Butler Yeats.

While sailing on July 8, 1822, Shelley's ship sank in a storm, and he drowned. Ten days later, Shelley's ruined body washed ashore near Via Reggio, Italy. Allegedly, a book of poems by John Keats was found in his coat pocket. On a miserably hot and humid day, his close friends Edward Trelawny, Leigh Hunt, and Lord Byron cremated Shelley's body on the beach. Shelley's ashes were buried in Rome, Italy.

## Further Study Questions

**Recall Questions**

1. What is the form of this poem called?
2. What is the central paradox of the poem?
3. In the first stanza, what main poetic device does Shelley use to try to describe the unseen power?

**Ponder Further**

4. Can you relate to Shelley's definition of intellectual beauty? Do you experience beauty as an emotional state, or do you have another definition? Express your ideas in your own ode to beauty.
5. Around the same time that Percy Bysshe Shelley wrote this poem, Mary Shelley wrote *Frankenstein*. Research the two authors. Jot down some facts and your ideas about their relationship. How do you think the two artists may or may not have inspired each other?

# 5

# "Ode on a Grecian Urn"

## John Keats (1795–1821)

John Keats began working as a medical apprentice at age fifteen. In a London hospital, he restrained surgery patients who had been given few painkillers or antiseptics. He bandaged wounds in a time when infection was rampant. Poetry helped him to endure the suffering and death that he faced. However, after he wrote his first poem, at age nineteen, Keats quit medicine altogether and devoted his life to writing. He would not have much time—he died at age twenty-five. The poems he wrote in those few short years would make him one of the best-known Romantic poets.

Keats never lived a life of luxury with lovely things around him. He escaped into his imagination to forget his harsh, ugly reality. In 1817, in a letter to a friend, he wrote: "What the

# John Keats

John Keats was born near London, England, on October 31, 1795, the oldest of four children to parents who owned an inn and a horse stable. His father was killed in a riding accident in 1804. When his mother contracted tuberculosis, Keats nursed her until her death in 1810. The fourteen-year-old was left impoverished and caring for his siblings. In 1811, he began to study medicine. In 1816, after becoming a licensed apothecary, or pharmacist, he abandoned medicine and changed his life's work to poetry. However, illness and tragedy continued to shape his life.

His beloved brother Tom grew sick with tuberculosis and died in December 1818. In 1819, Keats fell in love with Fanny Brawne. By then, however, he already had symptoms of tuberculosis. Two years later, in February 1820, though he knew his illness was most likely fatal, he traveled to Italy, hoping warmer weather would help him recover. He died in Rome, Italy, on February 23, 1821. He is buried in the city's Protestant Cemetery, and his tombstone is engraved with a line he requested: "Here lies one whose name was writ in water."

imagination seizes as Beauty must be truth." On a visit to the British Museum, Keats was amazed by an exhibit of sculptures from the Parthenon, an ancient temple dedicated to the Greek goddess Athena.

Afterward, Keats studied articles about Greek myths, art, and prints of Greek urns. He traced an engraving of a Greek vase from a book. The beauty of the ancient art made a deep impression on his imagination. In late 1819, Keats wrote "Ode on a Grecian Urn." The poem is probably based on an imagined urn but came from his response to the art. His poem was published in January 1820, in a London journal called *Annals of the Fine Arts*.

Twenty years after Keats died, a close friend, Charles Armitage Brown, wrote a short biography of the poet. He confirmed Keats's ability to absorb beauty into his imagination. "From his earliest boyhood," Brown wrote, "[Keats] had an acute sense of beauty, whether in a flower, a tree, the sky, or the animal world; how was it that his sense of beauty did not naturally seek in his mind for images by which he could best express his feelings?"

## Summary

The poem's speaker studies a Greek vase, or urn, and has a surprising experience. He speaks directly to this ancient piece of art. When he calls the urn an "unravish'd bride of quietness" and "foster-child of Silence and slow Time," he

## Ode on a Grecian Urn

*Thou still unravish'd bride of quietness,*
*Thou foster-child of Silence and slow Time,*
*Sylvan* historian, who canst thus express*
*A flowery tale more sweetly than our rhyme:*
*What leaf-fringed legend haunts about thy shape*
*Of deities or mortals, or of both,*
*In Tempe or the dales of Arcady?*
*What men or gods are these? What maidens loth?*
*What mad pursuit? What struggle to escape?*
*What pipes and timbrels? What wild ecstasy?*

*Heard melodies are sweet, but those unheard*
*Are sweeter; therefore, ye soft pipes, play on;*
*Not to the sensual ear, but, more endear'd,*
*Pipe to the spirit ditties of no tone:*
*Fair youth, beneath the trees, thou canst not leave*
*Thy song, nor ever can those trees be bare;*
*Bold lover, never, never canst thou kiss,*
*Though winning near the goal—yet, do not grieve;*
*She cannot fade, though thou hast not thy bliss,*
*For ever wilt thou love, and she be fair!*

*Ah, happy, happy boughs! that cannot shed*
*Your leaves, nor ever bid the Spring adieu;*
*And, happy melodist, unwearied,*
*For ever piping songs for ever new;*
*More happy love! more happy, happy love!*

*For ever warm and still to be enjoy'd,*
*For ever panting, and for ever young;*
*All breathing human passion far above,*
*That leaves a heart high-sorrowful and cloy'd,*
*A burning forehead, and a parching tongue.*

*Who are these coming to the sacrifice?*
*To what green altar, O mysterious priest,*
*Lead'st thou that heifer lowing at the skies,*
*And all her silken flanks with garlands drest?*
*What little town by river or sea shore,*
*Or mountain-built with peaceful citadel,*
*Is emptied of this folk, this pious morn?*
*And, little town, thy streets for evermore*
*Will silent be; and not a soul to tell*
*Why thou art desolate, can e'er return.*

*O Attic shape! Fair attitude! with brede*
*Of marble men and maidens overwrought,*
*With forest branches and the trodden weed;*
*Thou, silent form, dost tease us out of thought*
*As doth eternity: Cold pastoral!*
*When old age shall this generation waste,*
*Thou shalt remain, in midst of other woe*
*Than ours, a friend to man, to whom thou say'st,*
*"Beauty is truth, truth beauty"—that is all*
*Ye know on earth, and all ye need to know.*

*__sylvan:__ a rustic and spirit-like dweller of the woods.

connects the urn to the concepts of silence and time. Next, he calls it a "Sylvan historian," imagining the urn as a rustic, spiritlike dweller of the woods. Historians are dedicated to recording events truthfully. As a sylvan historian, the urn will be a mythical storyteller for the speaker. The vase will teach him something true. The vase also shows him the relationship of art to the imagination.

The clay vase, decorated with figures from Greek mythology, shows three scenes from the Greek myth of the god Pan. In the first scene, men and women play musical instruments, have a party, and laugh and chase each other. In the second scene, a man sits under some trees and plays music to serenade a woman he loves. He pursues her, "winning near the goal," but he will never reach her. The speaker tells this man not to worry or grieve. The man's hope of love will never fade, and the woman he loves will always be young and beautiful. The third scene is more somber. A procession of people prepare to sacrifice a cow to a god. A priest leads the cow that is about to be slaughtered. All the townspeople walk to the ritual. The town is empty and will always be silent.

The speaker concludes by contemplating his own death. He will grow old and die but the urn will remain just as it is. In that frame of mind, the speaker imagines the urn teaching humanity the mysterious lesson that "Beauty is truth, truth beauty."

## Explication

In "Ode on a Grecian Urn," Keats contrasts reality with art. Life changes. Art is permanent. The figures on the vase are stuck in one moment. They will never have to face loss, tragedy, or death, but they will never get to experience joy, love, or fulfillment. In contrast, the speaker's life will change a lot, from joy and happiness to loss, disappointment, and death. Even so, the unchanging urn shows him that beauty itself can be a human reality.

Each scene on the vase traps people at the height of intention. The frozen figures are just about to reach specific goals. The party is fun. The lovers see each other. The trees are blooming. The townspeople earnestly carry offerings to the gods. Keats seems to say that the figures are caught in the best moments. The people will never suffer any consequences of their actions. The lovers will never kiss, but they also will not break up. The trees will not lose their leaves. The citizens will not suffer tragedies that could make them feel abandoned by the gods. The figures are frozen at the height of hope and promise, free of human suffering.

No wonder the speaker begins to think about his own mortality. The figures on the urn are eternal. Being human is all about change. Love fades. Trees die. Faith can be shaken. The figures in art will never suffer "a heart high-sorrowful and cloy'd,/A burning forehead, and a parching tongue."

John Keats

After studying these images, the speaker has a revelation. He hears the urn's lesson. "Beauty is truth, truth beauty." It is hard to tell who speaks the next lines, whether it is the urn or the speaker, but they seem to interpret the lesson: "that is all/Ye know on earth, and all ye need to know." Over the years, critics and readers have endlessly debated the poem's last two lines. No one can fully agree on what they mean. If they mean that truth and beauty are the same, with no difference between them, then the reader still does not know what they are. They reflect each other but reveal nothing more about either quality. The mysterious lines encourage readers to interact with the poem the same way that the narrator interacted with the Greek urn.

In fact, Keats is aware that his poem is as unchanging as the urn. When he says the urn can "express/A flowery tale more sweetly" than his poetry, comparing visual images to his written lines, he seems to know that readers may contemplate his poem in the same way that he studied art. Just as he feels a longing when looking at the vase, he also seems to want to provoke longing in his readers.

When the speaker studied art, he mainly learned that what people can know on earth is limited. Even so, he still hopes to find beauty in eternity. In that way, he is like a figure on the urn, stuck in a sense of hope, at least while he lives. When he says, "All ye know on earth," he implies that there is a place beyond earth where there is more to know.

# Style, Technique, & Poetic Devices

To write this and other odes, Keats established his own poetic form. "Ode on a Grecian Urn" has five stanzas with ten lines each. Each line has ten syllables. The meter is iambic pentameter. The first four lines of each stanza form a simple quatrain, with the rhyme scheme *abab*. The following sestet, or section with six lines, has a more complicated rhyme scheme of *cdecde* and its variations. In this way, Keats merged the classical style represented by the ancient urn with a newer style of the Romantic era. Keats used this ten-line stanza, with the rhyme scheme *abab cdecde,* in his other odes as well.

Keats has a way of drawing the reader into the poem with his intimate tone, but he reveals nothing about himself in his work. The speaker's life circumstances are not important. The speaker's purpose is to connect the reader and the urn. In the first and fourth stanzas, notice that the speaker asks a series of questions. If the speaker poses questions to the vase, then the questions will never be answered. However, if the poem poses questions for readers, readers must engage in a conversation—with the vase! The vase "speaks" to the reader through its images of ancient Greek life, which the reader then interprets for himself or herself. The poem's meaning, then, comes from the reader's own reflection on art.

## Primary Quote: Keats's Writing Process

**Keats's friend Charles Armitage Brown helped Keats transcribe his poems from notes. According to Brown, Keats treated his notes carelessly. One day, in 1819, Keats sat outside writing for several hours. Brown recalled:**

> ***When he came into the house, I perceived he had some scraps of paper in his hand, and these he was quietly thrusting behind the books. On inquiry, I found those scraps, four or five in number, contained his poetic feeling on the song of our nightingale. The writing was not well legible; and it was difficult to arrange the stanzas on so many scraps. With his assistance I succeeded, and this was his Ode to a Nightingale, a poem which has been the delight of every one.***

## Thematic Relevance

Keats is considered one of the greatest poets of the Romantic era. Romantics, unlike Enlightenment thinkers, did not focus on science or reason. Reason could not measure concepts such as beauty and truth. Science could not explain the heart and soul. Mysterious qualities and sublime experiences fascinated Romantic poets. Keats saw beauty in sadness, and sadness in beauty, as he expresses in another poem about art, "Hyperion":

*"But oh! how unlike marble was that face:*
*How beautiful, if sorrow had not made*
*Sorrow more beautiful than Beauty's self."*

Keats wrote six important odes over a short time. They are considered exceptional. All the poems, including "Ode to Psyche," "Ode on Indolence," "To Autumn," and "Ode on a Grecian Urn" were published in Keats's 1820 collection, *Lamia, Isabella, Etc.*

He developed poetic stanzas in a way no one else ever had. After his beloved brother Tom died, Keats wrote "Ode to a Nightingale." Grief-stricken, Keats heard a birdsong in a garden and longed to escape his sorrow and loss. For him, the bird's song represented an ideal, clear beauty. The bird, part of nature, would change, but the song would last forever. The song jolted Keats to imagine leaving reality and living within the beauty of ethereal music.

In "Ode on Melancholy," Keats expressed a sense of melancholy, or sadness, that was heightened by beautiful things, and even though things fade, they reflect the principle of everlasting beauty. Loving beauty is bitter. The contrast between what is real and what is an ideal concept can be crushing. However, it is only because human beings feel so much that they suffer so much.

# Further Study Questions

**Recall Questions**

1. What helped inspire John Keats to write "Ode on a Grecian Urn"?
2. In the second stanza, what poetic device does Keats use to say that melodies "unheard/Are sweeter"?
3. What point does Keats make about the relationship between art and life?

**Ponder Further**

4. In what way does knowing that the urn is from ancient Greece help enrich the poem? How did the ancient piece of art guide Keats to state his mysterious conclusion? How do you interpret those last two lines of the poem?
5. Choose another one of Keats's six great odes to read. What ideas of beauty do you find in the poem?

# 6

# "Annabel Lee"

# Edgar Allan Poe (1809-1849)

Edgar Allan Poe thought poems themselves were beautiful. In his essay "The Poetic Principle," published in *Home Journal* in 1850, a year after his death, Poe defined poetry as "the rhythmical creation of beauty." Poe's taste in beauty, however, was not limited to the real world. True poets, he believed, created beauty to elevate the soul. They inspired a longing for the immortal. "Beauty of whatever kind in its supreme development invariably excites the sensitive soul to tears. Melancholy is thus the most legitimate of all the poetical tones," Poe wrote in his essay "The Philosophy of Composition," published in *Graham's Magazine* in 1846. Poe concluded, "The death then of a beautiful woman is unquestionably the most poetical topic in the world."

Merging death with beauty, Poe came up with twisted story lines and poem topics. He was called a Dark Romantic, and he wrote gothic fiction. During his life, he wrote sixty-six short stories, one play, one novel, and nine articles. His favorite genres were horror and suspense.

Before he wrote fiction, Poe wrote poetry. In 1827, he published fifty copies of *Tamerlane and Other Poems*. The book got very little attention. In 1829, he released another book of poems, and then he turned to writing fiction.

At age twenty-seven, Poe married his fourteen-year-old cousin, Virginia Clemm. They lived happily together until, five years later, Virginia contracted tuberculosis. For the next five years, she was constantly on the brink of death until she finally died in 1847. The years of her illness were hard on Poe's nerves. After her death, he sank into a severe depression.

The details of his own death are as horrific as one of his stories. After being found unconscious but sober on a Baltimore street, he spent four days in a hospital, drifting between clarity and delirium. He died on October 7, 1849, at age forty. Doctors at the time said he had brain congestion, but the cause of his death was a mystery. Based on his behaviors, some doctors today suggest he had contracted rabies.

# Edgar Allan Poe

Edgar Allan Poe was born in Boston, on January 19, 1809, the middle of three children. Their mother was a popular actress. Their father was a less successful performer. Poe spent his first two years among theatrical people. When he was two and a half years old, his life fell apart.

In August 1811, Poe's father left the family. His mother took the children to Virginia to perform in the Richmond Theatre. In October, she contracted tuberculosis. On December 8, she died. On December 26, the Richmond Theatre burned down, killing seventy-two people. Poe kept only two prized possessions, a portrait of his young mother and a picture of a theater. As he grew older, events became confused in his mind. He came to believe that both of his parents died in the tragic fire. Perhaps these events shaped Poe and gave him the "sensitive soul" of an artist.

Edgar Allan Poe

# Annabel Lee

*It was many and many a year ago,*
*In a kingdom by the sea,*
*That a maiden there lived whom you may know*
*By the name of Annabel Lee;*
*And this maiden she lived with no other thought*
*Than to love and be loved by me.*

I *was a child and* she *was a child,*
*In this kingdom by the sea:*
*But we loved with a love that was more than love—*
*I and my Annabel Lee;*
*With a love that the wingéd seraphs* of heaven*
*Coveted* her and me.*

*And this was the reason that, long ago,*
*In this kingdom by the sea,*
*A wind blew out of a cloud, chilling*
*My beautiful Annabel Lee;*
*So that her highborn kinsman came*
*And bore her away from me,*
*To shut her up in a sepulchre**
*In this kingdom by the sea.*

*The angels, not half so happy in heaven,*
*Went envying her and me—*
*Yes!—that was the reason (as all men know,*
*In this kingdom by the sea)*
*That the wind came out of the cloud by night,*
*Chilling and killing my Annabel Lee.*

*But our love it was stronger by far than the love*
*Of those who were older than we—*
*Of many far wiser than we—*
*And neither the angels in heaven above,*
*Nor the demons down under the sea,*
*Can ever dissever* my soul from the soul*
*Of the beautiful Annabel Lee:*

*For the moon never beams, without bringing me dreams*
*Of the beautiful Annabel Lee;*
*And the stars never rise, but I feel the bright eyes*
*Of the beautiful Annabel Lee;*
*And so, all the night-tide, I lie down by the side*
*Of my darling—my darling—my life and my bride,*
*In her sepulchre there by the sea,*
*In her tomb by the sounding sea.*

***seraphs:** angels

***covet:** to want or desire, often something that belongs to someone else

***sepulchre:** tomb

***dissever:** divide or sever

## Summary

The six-stanza poem has three distinct sections. In the first two stanzas, the poem's speaker vaguely states that whatever took place happened "many and many a year ago,/in a kingdom by the sea." He claims to have shared an amazing love with a young woman named Annabel Lee. They were not merely in love—they loved each other intensely.

In the next two stanzas, it seems that, exposed to harsh weather, Annabel Lee grew chilled and died. Her relatives came to retrieve her body, and they buried her in a grave. The speaker accuses angels in heaven of killing Annabel Lee with a cold wind. He claims they were jealous of the intensity of their love. He condemns her family for burying her. The family took her away from him, he says.

In the last two stanzas, the speaker mourns at Annabel Lee's grave. He still sees her everywhere, in his dreams and in the stars. Annabel Lee is dead, but their love is not. He still loves her so much that he goes and lies down with her in her tomb every night.

## Explication

The speaker loved a woman, and she died. It is a classic story. The genius of Poe's poem is in the narrator's delivery of the story. The speaker creates a twisted fairy tale that takes place in his mind. That Annabel Lee grew sick, died, and was buried are natural events. Naturally, her family wanted to bury her body. But for some reason, the narrator feels wronged. As he tries to blame natural events on supernatural forces, he falls apart. He tries to speak rationally, but he distorts the facts and reveals his "chilling" obsession. It becomes clear that he cannot distinguish reality from dream states.

The speaker explains a natural tragedy with supernatural cause and effect relationships. He uses logic as if he is on trial. However, he confuses the events, telling them out of context and out of order. "The reason" a cold wind blew was because he loved Annabel Lee. It wasn't simply harsh weather. He loved her "so that" her kinsman took her away. Because she got chilled, her kinsman shut her in a grave. He makes it sound as if her family buried her before she was dead. It is not until line 26 that the speaker is able to state the fact of Annabel Lee's death. He uses the word *killed,* not *died,* as if Annabel Lee had been murdered. Perhaps he cannot face the fact that she simply died of natural causes. The speaker is paranoid if he thinks the wind blew with malicious intentions and that her family buried her out of spite, to steal her away from him.

Readers will surely pity the speaker of "Annabel Lee." He lost his love. After a closer reading, however, readers might begin to distrust him. He is angry, distraught, and irrational. He leaves out a lot of concrete information. He might not be telling the truth, and he is certainly not telling the whole story.

In the third stanza, according to the speaker's version of the story, her family carried Annabel Lee away "[t]o shut her up in a sepulchre." So she is dead. But in the fourth stanza, the speaker rewinds to before Annabel Lee grew ill. Now he develops a new theory. Angels, not just a cold wind, stole Annabel Lee from him. Because he tells this part of the story after he says she is buried, it is a clue that perhaps his mind had grown unstable after her death. He needs to invent a cause for her loss. He again uses the word "reason." Clinging to a sense of logic, he says, "Yes!—that was the reason," but he sounds defensive, as if he knows that readers might doubt him. Indeed, his arguments sound suspicious.

In the final two stanzas, when he worships her at her grave, he gushes about Annabel Lee. He loves her even more now. The final stanza is where he falls apart. He is not grieving or sad. He no longer tries to be rational. He seems to have forgotten that he is telling someone else the story. Suddenly, he speaks in the present tense. His speech does not match his actions. He actively loves Annabel Lee, as if she were still alive, except that she is dead, and he must be lying in a literal or figurative murky graveyard alone. It seems like a dream, the ending more beautiful than the beginning, filled with the moon, the stars, and the night-tide. In this dramatic setting, he declares Annabel Lee beautiful twice. With his speech, he implies that death made her even more beautiful. With his actions, he shows that her death made him mad.

## Style, Technique, & Poetic Devices

Poe called "Annabel Lee" a ballad, a poem that tells a story and can be set to music. The poem contains elements Poe used often. In his short stories, he often created unreliable narrators, main characters whose actions conflict with their words or beliefs. They often are caught in their own lies and misperceptions. The narrator in "Annabel Lee" becomes unreliable. He believes in his own clarity, but his words also hint at a breakdown over the death of a beautiful woman.

The poem has a singsong rhythm and simple rhyme scheme. The lines alternate between four and three beats. The stanzas are slightly uneven, though. Some have six lines, while others have seven or eight. With devices such as repetition and an odd vocabulary, the narrator hints at crime but reveals insanity.

Poe uses fairy-tale language to deepen the story's unreality and to heighten its symbolism. The speaker calls Annabel Lee a maiden. He says *seraphs* instead of *angels, kinsman* instead of *family,* and *sepulchre* instead of *grave.* The opening line, "It was many and many a year ago," like the classic "Once upon a time," removes the story from any timeline. When did it happen? It could not have been that long ago if it was in the speaker's adulthood. And where is this "kingdom by the sea"? The word "kingdom" evokes images of royalty in castles ruling over peasant laborers. The sea, a powerful natural setting, is vast, empty, and, for the most part, inhospitable to humans. The tomb of Annabel Lee sits beside the water, between the kingdom and the sea. Time and place are not real.

Poe's use of repetition creates a hypnotic, mournful effect. Five times, the speaker chants the line "In this kingdom by the sea." With repetition, he overstates his love for Annabel Lee, asserts that angels killed her, and obsesses over her postmortem beauty. However, his repeated phrases lose meaning the more times he says them. Poe deliberately uses repetition not to stress story facts but to reveal the speaker's instability.

Poe uses repetition for an even craftier purpose, too. In a few places, the speaker changes the information slightly. By repeating the word "chilling," Poe implies two simultaneous meanings. Literally, Annabel Lee caught a chill in harsh weather. Figuratively, the event was chilling, meaning eerie and scary. Poe's devices work to dismantle the speaker. The speaker's emotional state takes over. If he cannot be trusted, readers have no framework to interpret his story. Readers do not know what to believe. Even in his last lines, it almost sounds as if the speaker lies down in her grave by the sea. Readers end up puzzled, less about Annabel Lee than about the stability of the speaker.

## Thematic Relevance

Published in 1841, Poe's short story, "The Murders in the Rue Morgue," is considered the first modern detective story. His poem "The Raven," printed in 1845, received great attention. People loved it. Poe wrote and sold "Annabel Lee" just before his death. The poem was published posthumously.

Annabel Lee and the unnamed narrator are fictional characters. However, some readers think the story comes from Poe's grief over the death of his wife, Virginia Clemm. Poe never admitted to it. He did not include autobiographical details in the poem. Critics and readers have called the poem beautiful and lyrical, simple and sweet, a fantastical story to embody the powerful emotions of love, sadness, and grief.

Another poem written after his wife's death, "Ulalume," may also have been inspired by her loss. Death and loss were not new themes for Poe. Death, especially of a beautiful woman, was one of Poe's favorite themes. He was a master at creating narrators in extreme states of mind. They are obsessed, terrified, enraged, or borderline insane. They become emotionally unhinged somehow and unable to distinguish reality from fantasy.

# Further Study Questions

**Recall Questions**

1. What is one of the devices that Poe uses to suggest symbolism?
2. What is one of the poetic devices that gives the poem a singsong quality?
3. How does the speaker believe Annabel Lee died?

**Ponder Further**

4. Do you agree with the explication in this chapter? Is there another way to interpret the poem? Consider an alternate interpretation. Jot your ideas in a brief paragraph. Make sure your ideas are based on details from the poem.
5. Online or in the library, find and read a copy of "The Raven," another of Poe's well-known poems. Compare "Annabel Lee" and "The Raven." How are the two poems alike and different?

7

# "In an Artist's Studio"

# Christina Rossetti (1830–1894)

Christina Rossetti lived in a family of poets, artists, and critics. The Rossetti home was a gathering place of artists. Christina's older brother, the poet and painter Dante Gabriel Rossetti, was close friends with artists William Holman Hunt, Ford Madox Brown, and John Everett Millais. In 1848, Dante was a key founder of a group of artists and writers called the Pre-Raphaelite Brotherhood.

Christina Rossetti sat as a model for her brother. His earliest sketch of her is from 1846. She was the model for the Virgin Mary in his first completed oil painting, *The Girlhood of Mary Virgin*. She sat for his artist friends as well. Rossetti must have known what it was like to be appreciated for her looks. She also saw and befriended some

Christina Rossetti

# In an Artist's Studio

*One face looks out from all his canvases,*
*One selfsame figure sits or walks or leans:*
*We found her hidden just behind those screens,*
*That mirror gave back all her loveliness.*
*A queen in opal or in ruby dress,*
*A nameless girl in freshest summer-greens,*
*A saint, an angel—every canvas means*
*The same one meaning, neither more or less.*
*He feeds upon her face by day and night,*
*And she with true kind eyes looks back on him,*
*Fair as the moon and joyful as the light:*
*Not wan with waiting, not with sorrow dim;*
*Not as she is, but was when hope shone bright;*
*Not as she is, but as she fills his dream.*

of the other women her brother painted and sketched. Her earliest poetry appeared in 1850, in the *Germ*, a magazine of the Pre-Raphaelites. She published *Goblin Market and Other Poems* in 1862 and *The Prince's Progress* in 1866.

In 1871, Rossetti was diagnosed with Graves' disease, a thyroid condition that changed her appearance, making her hair thin, her skin discolored, and her eyes appear to bulge. In 1877, she stopped sitting as a model for her portrait or photograph. By the 1880s, her illness kept her confined to home, but she continued to write poems and to socialize with her brothers' friends when they visited. Her social circle included artist James McNeill Whistler, English poet Algernon Charles Swinburne, and *Alice's Adventures in Wonderland* author Lewis Carroll.

## Summary

According to the title, this poem takes place in an artist's studio. Few details in the poem confirm this setting, but from the title, the reader can imagine paints, easels, canvas tarps, props, a painting smock, etc. The first line identifies three characters—the model ("her face"), the artist ("his canvases"), and the poem's narrator.

The male artist studies his model. The artist's model gets the most attention in the poem. She appears the most in the studio. She is behind screens, and she is reflected in a mirror. She is the subject of his paintings, where she sits,

# Christina Rossetti

On December 5, 1830, Christina Georgina Rossetti was born in London, the youngest of four children. Her father, the poet Gabriele Rossetti, was an Italian political exile who taught Italian at Kings College in London. Her mother was Frances Polidori, whose brother, John William Polidori, befriended Lord Byron in Italy in 1816. The Rossetti children, schooled at home, grew up speaking Italian and English. Rossetti also learned French, German, and some Latin. She was a healthy child until age fifteen, when she grew frail and delicate. She helped her mother teach in a series of day schools for young children. For ten years, from 1859 to 1870, she volunteered at St. Mary Magdalene's in Highgate, a charity house for former prostitutes and single mothers.

Rossetti was a devout Anglican, faithful to the Church of England. She had two important romantic relationships and both broke up over religious differences. She led a quiet life in her family home in London. She cared for her sister, Maria, who died in 1876; her brother Dante Gabriel, who died in 1882; and her mother, who died in 1886. The last years of her life were very quiet. Rossetti died of cancer on December 29, 1894.

walks, or leans, and is shown as a saint, angel, or queen, a nameless girl wearing different-colored dresses of blue, red, or green. Perhaps the artist likes how she looks. She may present a type popular for this era. It is not clear whether the artist paints one individual woman many times or if he paints all women to look alike. The artist, says the narrator, will not paint her as she is, but as he wants her to be.

## Explication

In this poem, a female narrator observes a male artist to write her poem. At the same time, the male artist uses a female model to create a painting. This is a poem about a woman studying a man who watches another woman. The narrator does not interact with the artist or model. She does not reveal herself. She never uses the pronoun "I." Instead, she says "we" at one point. Stating her point of view, she criticizes the point of view of the artist and his paintings.

Some of her opinion is strong, and some of it is subtle. At first, the narrator reveals her opinion through a subtle tone. The first four lines seem neutral. They make the studio seem pleasant. A lovely model appears behind a screen, in the canvases, and in the mirror. The model is different in each of the three places. Behind the screen, she is a real person, though slightly hidden. The paintings show her representation. And in the mirror, she is a reflection. The poem's fourth line says, "That mirror gave back all

## Brother and Sister

Rossetti closely read and championed the work of her brother, Dante Gabriel Rossetti, who published many lovely sonnets on the subject of beauty. In his book *The House of Life*, his sonnets have titles such as "Genius in Beauty" and "Love-Sweetness." In the lines below, he portrays a woman as soft and romantic:

*Sweet dimness of her loosened hair's downfall*
*About thy face; her sweet hands round thy head*

In 1881, Christina published a series of her sonnets called *Monna Innominata: A Sonnet of Sonnets*. Her poems give a voice to the woman idealized by male artists and authors in art and literature—women who were often portrayed as silent. In her preface, she states, "Had such a lady spoken for herself, the portrait left us might have appeared more tender."

Unlike her brother, who wrote about the act of winning love, Christina focused on unattained love. In her poems, her speakers never suffer disappointment because their desires are never fulfilled. With her first lines in "Sonnet 1," "Come back to me, who wait and watch for you: Or come not yet, for it is over then . . .," the speaker does not want seeing the one she loves to end her anticipation of that moment.

her loveliness." Does the narrator imply that the artist's canvases take it away or do not do her beauty justice?

In the next four lines, the narrator's tone becomes more cutting. The artist has placed the model in the glorified roles of queen, saint, and angel, always showing her with "[t]he same one meaning, neither more or less." It does not matter what role the model plays or what color she wears. She is not drawn as an individual woman with unique traits. She always looks the same. The narrator attacks the male artist when she says, "He feeds upon her face by day and night." She thinks the artist does not value the model except to serve his purposes and needs. She makes him sound greedy. It is not an attractive quality.

In line 10, she shifts her point of view to describe the model responding to the artist. The model is described as kind, true, and "fair as the moon and joyful as the light." There is no concrete information about the model. The narrator never really describes her. The artist might not portray the model as she really is, but neither does the poem's narrator. In the final two lines, she delivers her strong concluding message. The artist forces the woman into his view of her, the way he wants her to be, the way he thinks she should be. The narrator accuses the artist of making his model an object of his fantasies.

In this poem about art, Rossetti only uses the word "looks" twice; both times the model does the looking. "One face looks out" from the paintings, and "she with true kind eyes looks back on him." The model is patient, passive, and selfless. She exhibits behaviors appropriate for Victorian women of the time. If the artist uses her for his own purpose, the model seems to allow it. However, it is not the model the narrator criticizes—it is the artist. Rossetti's poem is a criticism of the way he makes art. It is a woman's interpretation of a man's interpretation of a woman's beauty.

## Style, Technique, & Poetic Devices

This is a sonnet, broken into two quatrains of four lines each and a sestet of six lines. Rossetti's end-rhymed scheme is *abba abba cdcdcd*. The lines are all written in iambic pentameter. Line 9 begins the sestet, the six-line section of the poem. In a sonnet using this structure, the sestet can introduce a new topic. Line 9 is where the sonnet changes or turns. Line 9 begins with the word "He" and is the only time the narrator directly describes the artist.

In the last lines of the sestet, the narrator uses the word "not" four times.

> ***Not*** *wan with waiting,* ***not*** *with sorrow dim;*
> ***Not*** *as she is, but was when hope shone bright;*
> ***Not*** *as she is, but as she fills his dream.*

The narrator describes what the model is not—not waiting, sad, or hopeful. She is not as she is. Instead, she

## Christina's Beauty

Christina Rossetti's brother William outlived her. In his brief memoir of his sister, which prefaced *The Poetical Works of Christina Georgina Rossetti*, his consideration of the question of her looks illustrates the attention she may have received. "She was certainly not what one understands by 'a beauty'; the term handsome did not apply to her, nor yet the term pretty. Neither was she 'a fine woman.' She has sometimes been called 'lovely' in youth; and this is true, if a refined and correct mould of face, along with elevated and deep expression, is loveliness."

William decided their brother Dante drew the best likeness of Christina in 1866. The likeness was exact, William believed, in spite of some critics' beliefs that his brother tended to idealize his subjects.

is romanticized, depicted the way she used to be "when hope shone bright," and romanticized in a way that fills the artist's dream. The word "dream," a near rhyme to "dim," could mean artistic vision. It could also mean fantasy or distortion of the truth.

In spite of the topic of art, there is not much clear, concrete imagery in the poem. This causes the reader to focus on human relationships, not the studio or any artwork. It is more a poem about ideas than images.

In most of the poem, the speaker makes an argument. The reader has to interpret her opinion based on her tone of voice. For example, when the narrator says, "He feeds upon her face," she makes him sound unattractive. Of course, he does not really devour or eat the model: it is a metaphor to describe how the artist looks at the model, a metaphor that Rossetti allows the reader to interpret.

## Thematic Relevance

As the subject of artists' sketches and paintings, Rossetti knew how it felt to be looked at for her physical beauty from an artist's point of view. Some critics interpret "In an Artist's Studio" as a commentary on the tendency of artists to objectify or idealize women. Scholars have linked Rossetti's poem to others on that theme, such as Robert Browning's "Andrea del Sarto," in which a male artist pretends to possess his estranged wife by asking her to pose as his model. In the story of Pygmalion from Ovid's *Metamorphoses,* a sculptor carves what he sees as the perfect woman. He falls in love with his own sculpture, meaning that what he is really in love with are his own ideas about women.

Rossetti's first book, *Goblin Market and Other Poems,* appeared in 1862, when she was thirty-one years old. It contains some of her best-known work. Her ballads and mystical poems are rich with symbolism and intense emotions. The book established her as a significant Victorian poet, one of the main female poets of her time. She was compared to Elizabeth Barrett Browning.

Rossetti's life and work were filled with loss. She suffered two romantic breakups and cared for many dying family members. Her sense of loss is reflected in her poems. Another poem about beauty, called "Beauty Is Vain," appeared in her next book, *The Prince's Progress and Other Poems,* in 1866. "Beauty Is Vain" is a no-nonsense take on the loss of physical appearance, a process she experienced in her illness.

# Further Study Questions

**Recall Questions**

1. In a sonnet, what is a sestet, and where does Rossetti's begin?
2. Other chapters have marked the meter of iambic pentameter. Choose one or two lines from the poem, and find the pairs of unstressed and stressed syllables. Mark the syllables that should be stressed.
3. Why didn't Rossetti include more description in her poem?

**Ponder Further**

4. The narrator says, "every canvas means/The same one meaning, neither more or less." What does she mean? How do you interpret her phrase, "the same one meaning"?
5. After you read this chapter, explicate another poem by Christina Rossetti on your own. Online or in the library, find and read a short poem by Rossetti, perhaps "Beauty Is Vain." In a paragraph or two, describe the message, argument, or opinion in the poem.

# 8

# "Beauty"

# Ella Wheeler Wilcox (1850–1919)

Ella Wheeler Wilcox became hugely popular in her time. She tended to write sentimental poems full of moral messages and simple advice on topics such as love, virtue, marriage, and behavior. Today, her most remembered lines, from her poem "Solitude," are "Laugh, and the world laughs with you,/Weep, and you weep alone." It is the kind of homespun wisdom found in many of her poems, as in the first stanza from her poem "Worth Living":

*I know not what the future may hold,*
*Or how to others it seems,*
*But I know my skies have held more gold*
*Than I used to find in my dreams.*

Her singsong rhymes and easy poetic forms appealed to mainstream audiences, but literary

# Ella Wheeler Wilcox

Ella Wheeler married Robert Wilcox in 1884. She and her husband had a loving marriage. They shared an interest in the occult and mystical phenomena concerning such topics as astrology, reincarnation, and life after death. They made a pact that whoever died first would reach out to the other and communicate from the spirit world, if possible. Robert Wilcox died of pneumonia in 1917.

After thirty years of marriage, Wilcox was grief-stricken by his loss. Months passed, and when she received no message from her dead husband, she grew frantic but found a way to calm her heart and mind. After that, she was convinced that her husband did try to speak to her. She died of breast cancer on October 30, 1919.

critics ignored her. Wilcox wanted to write entertaining poems that had wide appeal. She wanted to write for magazines that reached readers even in isolated rural areas like the prairie farm near Madison, Wisconsin, where she lived. Her family read Shakespeare, the Bible, and the poetry of Lord Byron, Robert Burns, and others. Occasionally, Wilcox had access to popular magazines and newspapers, and she devoured the current short stories and poems. To earn enough money to subscribe to those publications, she began to write the kind of items they published. Almost daily, she mailed stories and poems to magazine and newspaper editors, driving the family horse and buggy three miles to the post office. Her poems appeared in popular women's fashion magazines, such as *Godey's Lady's Book*, *Harper's Bazaar*, and the *Saturday Evening Post*.

Wilcox often stuck to the conventions of the time, which were particularly strict for women. For example, she advised women to be strong but not outspoken and to be proper by controlling desires. Women had high standards to live up to, as seen in the end of her poem "Womanhood":

*A sense of humor, and a touch of mirth,*
*To brighten up the shadowy spots of earth;*
*And pride that passes evil—choosing good.*
*All these unite in perfect womanhood.*

In spite of her conventionality, some of her popular poems became controversial. Her 1883 book *Poems of Passion* was banned by some readers and critics who found

# Beauty

*Though thy cheek be fair, as the roses are,*
*Thy brow like the drifted snow,*
*And thine eye as bright, as the diamonds light,*
*Yet if in thy heart doth grow*
*But noxious* weeds, and selfish deeds*
*Follow thy steps alway,*
*What in the end availeth* it, friend,*
*If thy face is fair, I pray.*

*For the smoothest brow, old Time will plow,*
*And he dimmeth the brightest eye;*
*And the fairest face, and the form of grace,*
*In the lowly grave must lie.*
*But our deeds live on, when life is done.*
*Nor Time, nor death destroy;*
*And the words we say, will make their way*
*With sorrow, or with joy.*

*And even the thought, that we utter not,*
*In heaven is like a shout.*
*And bad or good, it is understood,*
*And the angels write it out.*
*But they do not care, if the face be fair,*
*Or what the world deems plain.*
*They look to the heart, and the deathless part,*
*For the rest is poor and vain.*

***noxious:** toxic

***availeth:** benefits, advantages

her poems immoral. In the first poem in the book, "Love's Language," Wilcox described being in love: "How does Love speak?/By the uneven heart-throbs, and the freak/ Of bounding pulses that stand still and ache," she wrote. Words too sensual for some readers held great appeal for others. *Poems of Passion* became her biggest book, selling more than sixty thousand copies in its first two years.

## Summary

In "Beauty," the speaker states two opinions: physical looks fade with age, and good deeds last after death. She merges the two themes, implying that one topic has to do with the other. It is her opinion that character and personality are more important than how a person looks. Vanity is a downfall. She states a realistic truth about time, that youthful beauty fades as people grow older. The speaker adds a piece of moralistic opinion, however, when she says that good deeds do not fade, even after death. Angels in heaven record people's thoughts.

## Explication

With her single-word title "Beauty," it seems as if Wilcox might define the quality. Instead, she presents opinions about how to behave and how to feel about individual beauty. There are more important things in life than looks. Her tone is upbeat, and her advice sounds good, but it is not necessarily comforting. While her purpose may have been to calm fears of growing old, the poem expresses neither anguish nor joy. The narrator seems detached from genuine human emotion. This makes her words seem cold, and then even colder when she touches on a deeper fear than loss of beauty—the fear of death.

The narrator speaks with authority. She stresses the point that good deeds are more long-lasting than physical beauty, as if it is an either/or choice. Her authoritative tone does not leave room for interpretation. The speaker's tone is moralistic and preachy, in part because Wilcox does not identify or name her speaker. There is no "I" in the poem, no personal qualities, experiences, or problems. There is no sense that her speaker is a real individual. Wilcox also does not identify a specific audience. A generic speaker addresses a universal audience, which could be either male or female. At the time, it may have been assumed that she addressed a female audience, but her words could apply to men as well.

In the first stanza, the speaker poses a question. What use is beauty after death, especially if a person's deeds are selfish? At first, she addresses a single person, someone she refers to as "thy" and "friend." In stanzas 2 and 3, when she answers her question, she stops addressing "thy." She uses the first person plural "our" and "we." In stanza 2, she starkly opposes fading beauty and lasting good deeds, comparing their value after death. Beauty is destroyed while good deeds "live on."

## Fireside Poets

Ella Wheeler Wilcox wrote in a style similar to a small group of poets who wrote stirring, heartwarming poems about American life. The group earned the nickname "Fireside Poets" because their poems were often read aloud as families and friends gathered around the fire. The poets were also called "Schoolhouse Poets" because students recited their poems at public events. Popular verses included "Paul Revere's Ride" by Henry Wadsworth Longfellow, "Snow-bound" by James Greenleaf Whittier, "Old Ironsides" by Oliver Wendell Holmes, and "Oh Fairest of the Rural Maids" by William Cullen Bryant.

Readers must now imagine a world they no longer live in. Good deeds may live on, but people do not. In stanza 3, the speaker raises the stakes. She speaks of heaven and angels. Angels do not care about beauty and can hear a person's thoughts. She cautions readers against negative thinking. In a time when women's external actions and behaviors were repressive, she advocates for more control. Women should not even have negative private thoughts.

Again, the speaker has a voice of authority. She does not explain how she came to this knowledge about angels. Perhaps they were sentiments she believed, but they were also mysteries she could not verify. She states them with conviction. Wilcox assumed that her readers would accept ideas like that, even if the literary critics rejected them. She repeated common beliefs of her time. When a person dies, beauty dies and good deeds live on. That's all there is to it. Readers of her day, however frightened, might have found this to be solid advice.

## Style, Technique, & Poetic Devices

"Beauty" is divided into three stanzas. Each stanza has an "if/but" structure to make an argument. In the first four lines, the speaker sets up an argument. Then, notice that every fifth line begins with the word "But." The conjunction indicates a turn of thought. In the last four lines of each stanza, Wilcox argues against the first four lines. In the first stanza, you might be beautiful, *but* beauty is nothing if you are not a good person. In the second stanza, beauty disappears after death, *but* words and deeds live forever. In the third stanza, angels record people's words, *but* they do not care about looks.

Wilcox gave "Beauty" a singsong melodic rhythm. For the most part, each line contains a complete phrasing or thought. The first line has four beats. The second line has three beats. The rest of the lines have the same alternating meter. Each eight-line stanza has two quatrains, or sets of four lines. The stanza rhyme scheme is *abcb defe*. Only the even numbered lines share an end rhyme. But notice that most of her four-beat lines also contain a rhyme in the line itself. For example, in the line "And thine eye as bright, as the diamonds light," the words "bright" and "light" rhyme. Her internal rhyme enforces the poem's singsong quality.

Critics found Wilcox's metaphors and similes unsophisticated. In her era, to compare cheeks to roses was growing cliché. Her metaphor for time is crude. "For the smoothest brow, old Time will plow," she says, as if time is a farmer and a person's forehead a dirt field. Perhaps the words "brow" and "plow" simply made an easy rhyme. Her simile is like one of Shakespeare's, the first lines of "Sonnet 2": "When forty winters shall besiege thy brow,/And dig deep trenches in thy beauty's field . . ." Wilcox may have borrowed the idea to describe the wrinkles of old age.

## Thematic Relevance

One of Ella Wheeler Wilcox's jobs was to write a syndicated newspaper column, giving advice on morals and manners to a national audience. She often responded to her readers' concerns about their looks. Wilcox's role as advice-columnist

# Late Nineteenth-Century Roles

Wilcox was forty-three years old when the World's Columbian Exposition in Chicago opened in 1893. Also called the World's Fair, the event included the Woman's Building Library. The women on the planning committee gathered as complete a collection of women's literature as they could. Among more than seven thousand books was Wilcox's *The Beautiful Land of Nod*. Today, that list of books reflects women's perceptions of women's roles, at least in those writings, of the late nineteenth century.

Though change would come slowly, the exhibits, presentations, and art of the Woman's Building Library increased awareness of the need for women's rights. By the time World War I ended, the image of the flapper replaced the Gibson Girl. No more tight girdles, wide skirts, or long fussy hair. No more staying home and being proper. Women began to express contempt and frustration with conventional enforced behaviors.

also slipped into her poetry. "Beauty" appeared early in her career, in her second book, *Shells* (1870). It was a time when men and women focused on appearance. A person's beauty could be a subject of social and even public debate. Ideas about beauty helped to shape acceptable behaviors. Much like today, people were judged according to their clothing and hairstyles, as well as manners of walking, sitting, speaking, etc.

Wilcox wrote in a time when women's roles in society were changing and were about to change very dramatically. In 1890, artist Charles Dana Gibson drew an idealized image of a woman, called the Gibson Girl. Many women, including Wilcox, were influenced by this image. With upswept hair, a narrow waist, and a long skirt, the Gibson Girl set new trends in fashion and attitude. Even though the Gibson Girl still wore long skirts, girdles, fancy hats, and gloves, the image helped women cross gender barriers. For example, women could be more athletic and have fun in public by roller-skating, golfing, and riding bicycles.

Like the Gibson Girl, Wilcox's strong-minded speakers valued manners. They were never aggressive, pushy, or angry. Her columns, printed in a book called *A Woman of the World: Her Counsel to Other People's Sons and Daughters* (1904), were meant to encourage and comfort a mainstream audience. In one column, called "To the Sister of a Great Beauty," Wilcox consoled a reader who was insecure about her looks. She ended with this advice:

"There is nothing a woman with youth, will-power, and *love* may not accomplish—even to the convincing of the world that she is beautiful, when her mirror may say otherwise."

Ella Wheeler Wilcox published forty books. During her lifetime, she saw only the beginning of the women's movement. At the time of her death, in 1919, a new generation of women poets had emerged in the Modern era, including Edna St. Vincent Millay, Louise Bogan, and Marianne Moore. When World War I ended, more and more women joined the workforce and pursued higher education. Women sought to fulfill rather than suppress artistic, intellectual, and occupational goals. The poetry of Ella Wheeler Wilcox, so very popular during her time, lost relevance and faded from public interest.

## Further Study Questions

**Recall Questions**

1. In your own words, what statement does the poem make about beauty?
2. What is an example of a line containing only three beats?
3. How is each stanza structured?

**Ponder Further**

4. Ella Wheeler Wilcox was popular during her lifetime but not after her death. Why do you think a poem like "Beauty" appealed to a popular audience but not to literary critics, scholars, or the next generation of readers? In what ways might her poetry appeal to readers today?
5. Poet Edna St. Vincent Millay (1892–1950) was popular in the Modern era. Like Wilcox, Millay was publically scrutinized for being an artistic, successful woman. Read a brief biography of Millay and a selection of her poems, perhaps online at the Academy of American Poets Web site, <www.poets.org> or the Poetry Foundations Web site, <www.poetryfoundation.org>. How are themes in Millay's poetry similar to or different from Wilcox's? How much of this comparison can be attributed to the context of her time?

# Sample Answers to Further Study Questions

**Note:** Answers to questions that ask for reader opinions will vary. There is no one correct answer. Responses should, however, demonstrate a close reading of texts.

## CHAPTER 1: "Sonnet 18"

**William Shakespeare (1564–1616)**

1. The *a*-words are *day* and *May*. The *b*-words are *temperate* and *date*.
2. It is the place where the topic changes. The poet stops describing nature's changes and talks about immortalizing beauty in writing.
3. Death is said to be able to brag, even though death is not a person and cannot speak.
4. Responses will vary. The themes in "Sonnet 54" are similar to "Sonnet 18." The older poet describes the beauty and flaws in nature, this time in a rose. The sweetest roses are beautiful because they are loved and not ignored. He once again praises his own skills, both his writing and his ability to love.
5. Responses will vary.

**CHAPTER 2: "To S.M. a Young African Painter, on Seeing His Works" Phillis Wheatley (1753–1784)**

1. Moral behaviors and qualities, such as honesty, nobility, truth, and virtue, represented beauty because they aligned with Puritan values and Wheatley's Christian faith.

2. Scipio Moorhead, an African-American artist and an enslaved man. He was a friend and neighbor of Wheatley's.

**Image:** Wheatley is not looking at the viewer. Shown in profile, she lifts her eyes, thinking about what she writes. She has a slight smile. Her cap matches her dress. She wears an apron, perhaps a symbol of her identity as a house slave. She wears a cord around her neck—a necklace?

**Art Style:** I like the artist's use of shading. He made light space around her head. He chose an oval frame, and made the table and chair rounded. There are no sharp edges or right angles in the drawing.

3. The reward of deeply thinking is that your soul is uplifted.

4. Responses will vary. A drawing like Scipio Moorhead's can be taken in all at once. Viewers can look more deeply into the single, whole image and see its positive point of view, the intention to delight viewers and illustrate Wheatley's strengths. Poetry, such as Wheatley's poem, must be absorbed line by

line. Her vision is expressed by multiple images. It is up to the reader to understand and interpret the single, whole idea of the poem.

5. Responses will vary. Contemporary poets have more freedom than Wheatley did to express anger. Their purpose is often to promote change. Wheatley's purpose seems to have been to praise things as they are or were.

**CHAPTER 3: "She Walks in Beauty"**
**Lord Byron (1788–1824)**

1. In lines 5 and 6, the words *mellowed, tender,* and *heaven* all have the same short "e" sound. In line 9, *waves* and *raven* are slant rhymes. The word *every* repeats the "v" sound. In line 11, the sibilant phrase "serenely sweet express" contains the "s" and long "e" vowel sounds.

2. Both similes compare beauty to time and aspects of nature. Daytime, bright and sunny, makes beauty seem obvious and clear. Night is dark, wild, and sleepy. Night makes beauty mysterious and hard to see or define.

3. The poem is not about one person; it tries to capture the unearthly beauty of balanced light and dark.

4. Responses will vary. Even though the speaker does not call attention to himself, the poem is all about his own response, not someone else's beauty.

5. Responses will vary. His curly hair and handsome face make him look athletic. He almost looks like

a Shakespearean actor. He is also shown in deep thought. The picture captures his intelligence.

### CHAPTER 4: **"Hymn to Intellectual Beauty"**
**Percy Bysshe Shelley (1792–1822)**

1. An ode.
2. The narrator tries to describe a power that is indescribable, and/or because he is human, he longs to understand the "unseen power," but because he is human he will never understand it.
3. Simile. He writes five similes, images he compares to the unseen power using the words *like* or *as*.
4. Responses will vary.
5. Responses will vary. Mary Shelley and Percy Bysshe Shelley were both highly imaginative. Mary got the idea for *Frankenstein* from a dream.

### CHAPTER 5: **"Ode on a Grecian Urn"**
**John Keats (1795–1821)**

1. Keats saw a museum exhibit, studied Greek art in books, and traced a picture of an urn.
2. Oxymoron, or paradox.
3. Art never changes. It represents a form of eternity. Life is always changing, but people can learn from art how to live.
4. Responses will vary. The urn is ancient. It is centuries old and from a different time. Society now looks

nothing like the world represented on the urn. It supports Keats's point that life changes but not art.

5. Responses will vary. In "Ode to Psyche," the speaker imagines he sees Cupid and Psyche in the woods. He has a sort of dream. The speaker is drawn into his vision of the beauty of the Greek goddess. He thinks if he worships her, she will be real and he can love her. He forgets the reality of his own era. An imagined beauty makes him forget who he is.

### CHAPTER 6: "Annabel Lee" Edgar Allan Poe (1809–1849)

1. The language of fairy tales and/or structure of allegory.
2. The meter, end rhyme, and use of repetition.
3. He thinks angels sent a chilling wind because they were jealous of his love for her.
4. Responses will vary. Annabel Lee had many connections. She had the speaker, the angels, and her family. She was connected to nature, religion, and society. The speaker seems to have no one except Annabel Lee. He is not stable. He is intensely lonely and alone.
5. Responses will vary. Like "Annabel Lee," "The Raven" has repetition and a rolling, singsong rhythm. "The Raven" is longer, but it also shows the speaker going through a change in his mind because of a lost love. He starts out rational, sitting and reading. In a fantasy

conversation with a bird, the speaker does most of the talking. He grows increasingly emotional, like the speaker in "Annabel Lee."

**CHAPTER 7: "In an Artist's Studio"**
**Christina Rossetti (1830–1894)**

1. A sestet is the final six-line section of a sonnet. It can be the place where a new idea is introduced. Rossetti's begins in line 9, with the word "He."

2. Here is an example of two lines from the poem in which the stressed syllables are marked:

˘ / ˘ / ˘ / ˘ / ˘ /
One **face** looks **out** from **all** his **can**vases,

˘ / ˘ / ˘ / ˘ / ˘ /
One **self**same **fig**ure **sits** or **walks** or **leans**.

3. One reason is that her poem is about the artist's ideas, not his images. She wanted to assert her opinion, not describe pretty images like the artist does.

4. Responses will vary. The narrator thinks that the artist's point of view is limited. He cannot see a woman as an individual. Her point is that his "same one meaning" is shallow. His paintings never reveal anything deeper. They do not show his model's complexities, her darker side, of waiting, disappointment, and sadness, etc.

5. Responses will vary. The title, "Beauty Is Vain," expresses the poem's opinion. Rossetti compares

a woman to a flower. Her point is that if a woman values herself only for beauty, she might as well be like a flower. She can look pretty, be admired, and be subject to the seasons. The ending opinion is abrupt. The woman is still going to die. Rossetti implies that a life devoted to physical appearance is shallow and wasted. She does not provide an alternative way to live. She just says beauty is vain and implies that vanity is a vice, not a virtue.

### CHAPTER 8: **"Beauty"**
**Ella Wheeler Wilcox (1850–1919)**

1. Beauty, as in physical good looks, does not last, does not matter, and is vain.
2. Line 4 in the second stanza: "In the lowly grave must lie." All the even-numbered lines have three beats.
3. Each stanza, composed of two quatrains, has the rhyme scheme *abcbdefe*.
4. Responses will vary. It sounds as if Wilcox did not try to sound scholarly. Her poem is easy to understand. It provides guidance rather than provokes thought. It does not require the reader to think as hard as a scholar. Today, readers could enjoy Wilcox's poems and see them as a representation of a historical era, one that was on the brink of change.
5. Responses will vary. Like Wilcox, Edna St. Vincent Millay was a society "it" girl. Like Wilcox, she represented attitudes of her time about women.

Those attitudes shaped the kind of poets Wilcox and Millay became. In Wilcox's time, women were proper. In Millay's time, women risked being improper. One difference is that Wilcox reached mainstream audiences while Millay appealed more to literary audiences. Millay's poems are more lyrical and not as straightforward.

# Glossary

**alliteration**—The repetition of initial consonant or vowel sounds shared by closely placed words or phrases.

**ballad**—A poem that includes elements of songs and folktales.

**couplet**—A pair of end-rhymed lines.

**end rhyme**—A pattern made when the last word of a line of poetry sounds the same as the last word in other lines of the same poem.

**explication**—A detailed explanation of a text; an analysis or interpretation that explains meaning.

**foot**—A rhythmic unit of verse made up of various patterns of unstressed and stressed syllables.

**heroic couplet**—A pair of end-rhymed lines that are written in iambic pentameter and are closed, forming a single complete thought and coming to a grammatical end.

**iamb**—A metrical foot consisting of an unstressed syllable followed by a stressed syllable.

**internal rhyme**—Rhyme created by two or more words in the same line of verse; rhyme created by words in the middle of two or more lines of verse.

**lyric poem**—A short poem with songlike qualities, such as rhyme and meter, imagery, and intense personal emotion.

**metaphor**—A figure of speech in which an object or action is compared to another to suggest similarity between them.

**meter**—The measure of rhythm in a line of poetry; a pattern of stressed and unstressed syllables in a line.

**ode**—A longer lyric poem expressing exalted emotions on a single subject, with lines of varying lengths and complex rhythms.

**pentameter**—A line of verse with a meter of five stressed beats.

**personification**—A literary device in which human attributes are applied to inanimate objects.

**quatrain**—A stanza of four lines, usually with alternating end rhymes of *abab*.

**rhyme**—A pattern made when two or more words sound identical except for their first letters or syllables.

**rhyme scheme**—A formal pattern of rhymes in a stanza or poem; noted by letters, pairs of rhyming lines might show a rhyme scheme of *aabb* while alternating rhyming lines might show a rhyme scheme of *abab*, etc.

**satire**—In a literary composition, using irony, sarcasm, and ridicule to expose and comment on, for example, human vice or weakness; a parody.

**sestet**—A six-line section of verse with a specific rhyme scheme.

**sibilance**—A hissing sound made with words using the consonants “s” and “z.”

**simile**—A figure of speech in which two things are compared using the words *like* or *as*.

**slant rhyme**—Words that share some but not all vowel or consonant sounds.

**stanza**—A grouping of lines in a poem, often separated by a line space, similar to a paragraph in prose writing.

**sublime**—Lofty, grand, or exalted in thought, expression, or manner.

**symbolism**—A image that represents or stands for another quality or meaning; also a late nineteenth-century movement in French art and literature in which objects had symbolic meaning.

# Further Reading


Andronik, Catherine M. *Wildly Romantic: The English Romantic Poets—The Mad, the Bad, the Dangerous.* New York: Henry Holt and Co., 2007.

Mussari, Mark. *Poetry*. New York: Marshall Cavendish Benchmark, 2011.

Parisi, Joseph, and Stephen Young, eds. *The Poetry Anthology*. Chicago: Ivan R. Dee, 2004.

Pockell, Leslie, ed. *100 Essential American Poems*. New York: Thomas Dunne Books, 2009.

Wroe, Ann. *Being Shelley: The Poet's Search for Himself.* New York: Pantheon, 2007.

# Internet Addresses

**The Poetry Foundation: Poems & Poets**
<http://www.poetryfoundation.org/browse/>

**Poets.org: Poems for Teens**
<http://www.poets.org/viewmedia.php/prmMID/20785>

# Index